Arthur Konyot:

The White Rider

My 60 Years as a Circus Equestrian

as told to

William D. Reichmann

The Hill and Dale Press
Barrington, Illinois

First Printing

PRINTED IN THE UNITED STATES

Illustrations by Elizabeth Mihalyi

Arthur Konyot:
The White Rider

Dedication

To the memory of Adolph Konyot,
skilled equestrian, bareback rider, animal trainer,
soldier, and gentleman.

ARTHUR KONYOT.

Contents

Foreword

THE INTRODUCTION which led to my becoming acquainted with Arthur Konyot came about in an accidental way at the 1949 International Live Stock Exposition & Horse Show in Chicago. Ruth "Bazy" McCormick Tankersley of Washington, D.C., the moving spirit behind a pageant of Arabian horses at the Chicago show that year, introduced me to John F. Cuneo, Jr., a Chicagoan, and in the conversation which followed Mr. Cuneo said:

"I know one of the greatest horse trainers in the country. He is right here in Chicago and I think it would be worth your while to have a talk with him. If it is all right with you, I will bring him out here to your stalls in the morning."

That is what he did, and the next day I went with him to the Ambassador Stables on Chicago's North Side to watch Arthur Konyot train and ride. This resulted in my placing the young Arabian stallion Kamlah in the latter's hands and to the association which led to my becoming the narrator of these reminiscences.

From 1950 until 1954 Arthur Konyot conducted a Riding Academy & School of Equitation at 1501 North Clark Street, Chicago, and it was there that I began taking down the story of his eventful and dramatic life. The Konyots—Arthur, his wife, Manya, and their son and daughter, Alexander and Dorita, came to the United States from Paris in 1940. They came with a big reputation. Arthur's center ring performances in the Ringling Brothers and Barnum & Bailey Circus, in which he rode the high-school, put him in the limelight here. It was known that he and his family had passed through some harrowing experiences during their last months in Eastern Europe. As a likely prospect for

ix

a good news story, Arthur Konyot was interviewed a number of times. But these were just random, on-the-spot interviews with the accent on a few highlights and little more.

Here was an extraordinary man, as every line in his immensely strong and eloquent face indicated. At 62 he had the vitality and the erect carriage of a man half his age. The impact of his lively and magnetic personality was decisive. And what abilities! A stellar member of the great Konyot troupe of bareback riders and a juggler on horseback in his younger days, he was a circus equestrian and high-school exhibitionist of the top rank. He was an animal trainer in the broad sense and could train an elephant, a camel, a kangaroo, a donkey, a poodle, a pig, or a monkey, all these, and more, with equal facility. That this man had a fascinating story to tell was known by many. Yet no one had bestirred himself to get that story. It became my aim to do so, and to take it down from the beginning.

From the clatter and hubbub of Chicago's North Clark Street at the Riding Academy, where we got under way, and later from the comparative quietude of the old Virginia homestead on Arthur Godfrey's Beacon Hill Farm near Leesburg, where the Konyots lived from 1954 until early in 1960, I was taken far afield. In recapturing the memories of his long and notable career, Arthur Konyot had to re-live his life. I accompanied him on the journey, shared with him his visions of many a remembered scene in as many lands, felt myself present in the gay and happy days of his youth in the family circus and experienced with him the difficulties met and overcome, his trials and triumphs down through the years.

There were some hard and bitter times in this man's life, times when hearts less stout might have despaired, but high courage and indefatigable enterprise won the day. All in all, it has been a delightful, very entertaining, and rewarding journey in the companionship of warm-blooded people who were gay and brave, a two-dimensional voyage in time and space—with musical overtones—the action taking place against the background of historic happenings in our time.

It now becomes my pleasure to make some acknowledgements. I wish to express my gratitude to Ed and Janie Jenkins of Youngstown, Ohio, warm friends and admirers of Arthur Konyot, and of mine, and to "Bazy" Tankersley for encouragement in this endeavor. I thank the friends of Arthur Konyot from the circus world, who came forward with programs and other material, and their own recollections, which were of help to him in clarifying his memories. To Oscar and Patricia Konyot of Sarasota, Florida, I am grateful for material and pictures, and I thank Lilly Reinsch Konyot, Adolph Konyot's widow, and Dorita K. Humphreys for similar assistance. For editorial counsel and advice I am indebted to Van Allen Bradley of Chicago and Barrington, Illinois, and for courtesies extended I thank the Newberry Library of Chicago. Last, but not least, I express my gratitude to Elizabeth Ann Konyot, Arthur Konyot's wife, and to my sister, Harriette R. Forrest, for their faith and helpfulness beyond compare.

                                        WILLIAM D. REICHMANN

Barrington, Illinois
August 3, 1961

PHOTOGRAPHIC CREDITS Most of the photographs in this book come from the private collections of the Konyot family A number are official circus photographs, particularly the Ringling Brothers and Barnum & Bailey items In some cases it was impossible to identify sources, and the authors express herewith a blanket "Thank you" for their use They also wish to credit the following specific sources for permission to use certain of the pictures To John Eisenhart of the Loudon (Virginia) Times-Mirror for the picture, "first lessons between the pillars", to Lloyd Jones of the Youngstown (Ohio) Vindicator for the picture of Arthur Konyot and Pluto, and to M E Morris of Centralia, Illinois, for the photograph of Arthur Konyot and Kamlah at Indianapolis

Arthur Konyot:
The White Rider

Prologue

A Circus Came to Rajec

One day in the late 70's of the last century a circus came to Rajec, Hungary. It was one of many wandering circuses that took to the road every spring in Europe and the Balkans and with feats of skill and daring, performing animals, and assorted wonders to behold lightened the hearts of the young and old in city, town, and village across the far-ranging land. In Europe, as in America, interest ran high when the circus came to town, and so it was this day in Rajec. The arrival there of this circus occasioned an interest that was exceptional, however.

Twelve years before, almost to the day, a 15-year-old Rajec boy had run away from home to enter that beckoning world apart, the circus. No one had heard from him in all the passing years, though he was reported to have made good, to the extent, even, of having married a beautiful equestrienne, who was the daughter of a famous circus owner. And rumor now had it that the proprietor of the circus that had just come to Rajec was none other than that same runaway boy. When the identity of this man of the circus had been established and the reports about him were verified, the townspeople flocked to the circus grounds to have a look at him and to claim him as their own. Leopold Konyot, the man who was to become my father, learned what it is like to be feted as a hero.

Grandfather Konyot was an exacting parent and had decided in his own mind just what his sons were to do with their lives.

1

*He had been amused when Leopold, at the age of 10, an-
nounced his intention of becoming a circus performer, but he
had ceased to be amused when the boy, in his 14th year, continued to proclaim that purpose and predicted that the day
would come when he would have a circus of his own. Grandfather Konyot had now had enough of such talk. Leopold
would do what his older brothers were doing, he declared. He
would continue his schooling in preparation for one of the pro-
fessions, such as the law, medicine, teaching, or banking. The
circus? Nonsense! The very thought of it outraged him. If the
vehemence with which his father expressed himself on this
subject had had any effect on young Leopold, other than to
strengthen his resolve, that effect was only temporary. For, in
the following spring, when the Zirkus Kleber took down its
tents, after a few days in Rajec, and rolled away, the boy went
with it.*

*For five years the young runaway traveled all over Europe
and the Balkans with the Zirkus Kleber, and rose from the status
of a mere errand boy and stable groom to become an acrobat
and an aerialist. At the age of 20, he was taken on by the larger
and more important circus of the Blumenfeld Brothers, under
whose tutelage he became skilled in the training and presentation of liberty horses. In his 21st year he won the heart of the
proprietor's daughter Henrietta, who became my mother.*

*The distress this defiant youth had brought upon his parents
led to an estrangement, which hardened over the years, and, so
far as father and son were concerned, was not subject to recon-
sideration. Grandfather Konyot was informed of Leopold's
return to Rajec as a full-fledged circus proprietor, but he was a
stubborn man and could not find it within himself to forgive
and forget. With my uncles it was otherwise. They went at
once to the circus to greet their young brother and prevailed
upon him to go to his father's house, and when Grandfather
found himself confronted with the countenance and manly
presence of his youngest son, he gave way to an overwhelming
emotion and with his whole heart cried out, "My son!"*

I

My Home Was on Wagon Wheels

The Cirkus Leopold

LIKE MOST people of old circus parentage, I was born on the road. On Dec. 9, 1888, the day of my birth, our caravans were at the city of Sopron, near the Austrian frontier, in Hungary, my homeland. Of greater consequence, however, was the circumstance of being born in the circus. Circus folk of the old traditions lived, as they traveled, in wagons, and I drew my first breath in the wagon that was my parents' home. My earliest memories are of a big round tent and wagons that were red and white, of horses and ponies, acrobats, clowns, and dancing bears, and of the Ring, sometimes referred to as "the Charmed Circle," on which, as I early came to understand, the whole life of the circus converged and the efforts and ambitions of all of us were centered. In the foreground of my memories are the horses and ponies, the beat of their hoofs upon the ground, their neigh-

3

ing and nickering, and the feel of their coats. My boyhood recollections of the great world around us yield up a somewhat blurred panorama of varied and changing scenery, with the focus on a more immediate phenomenon, the ever demanding, ceaselessly wandering little world in which all of us, my parents, five brothers, six sisters, and I, had our being, working, learning, struggling, enjoying life, and, within its confines, achieving together the Cirkus Leopold.

Ours was typical of the comparatively small, family-owned traveling circuses of the last century from which so many of the famous *artiste* clans of the past have come. The Blumenfelds, my mother's family, were such a clan. Through them we Konyots descend by way of four generations from the early 18th century bareback rider and rope-dancer Goldkette, founder of the numerous circus clans of that name and a number of off-shoots thereof. Specifically, the tradition in which we had our roots was that of bareback riding, which involved the ability to perform acrobatics on the back of a cantering or galloping horse and to jump on and off the horse or from one horse to another. For this a rigorous training was essential, and it began early. First lessons in ballet and tumbling and on the trapeze began at four or soon thereafter, and we were put on the backs of ponies at about the same age. My father, who had been an acrobat, a contortionist, and an aerialist, saw to it that we all had this early training, and my mother, distinguished in her day as a bareback rider, never ceased to stress the indispensability of ballet training as the medium through which to acquire the art of graceful presentation, which is showmanship.

"When you have learned what to do with your hands and feet," she used to say, "the rest will come naturally. It is not only what you do, but how you do it that is important." My mother was proud of the tradition in which she was reared and endeavored to instill that same pride in us.

Conditions were comparatively primitive in the days of my youth. Illumination was by the kerosene and carbide lamp, and the hauling and pulling, of course, was done by horses. The

Cirkus Leopold was still a wagon show, by which I mean that we had not yet taken to the rails in transporting our caravans. Draft horses were available for hire in most European towns and cities in that day, and, while we always had some work teams or baggage stock of our own, we hauled our caravans from place to place with rented horses, and in that manner traveled over the long-trodden highways and byways of Austria-Hungary, Germany, and the Balkans. To be mired down in mud after long rains and to have to face into clouds of wind-borne dust for days on end, not to mention many other difficulties and hardships, was the lot of those who followed the road. The stands we made in the course of these almost continuous peregrinations were customarily for three or four days to a week at the provincial towns and cities. In the winter, however, we remained at one location for longer periods and frequently for the season. The winter stands were in permanent circus buildings and auditoriums, or in frame structures erected by contractors for a percentage of the gate receipts. The latter we heated with coke in iron drums.

As one of my generation reflects upon it, the realization comes that there was a certain buoyancy to life and living in Europe before 1914 that went out of the world with the coming of the first World War. Circus folk, it is true, have not lost their courage nor their capacity to persevere, but they have been deprived of that unquestioning belief in the future which was so real before 1914 and which made for continuity within the circus families, in adherence to the great traditions. My parents were strong in that fortitude and they imbued the rest of us with something like it. It follows that as a large and united family we were equipped to stand firm and make a fight of it, should trouble come our way, and it did.

Catastrophe on a Summer Day

It happened on a summer day at a small town on the Great Hungarian Plain, to which the Cirkus Leopold had come for a

66666666   ARTHUR KONYOT: THE WHITE RIDER

two-day stand. The name of the place has been well forgotten, but what happened there has not been. Townsfolk and peasants from the region around were streaming out to the meadow, where we had pitched our tents. The pennons on the center poles fluttered in the breeze, and the band was playing. The interval between gate opening and the grand entry had arrived, and our bareback horses, bridled and surcingled, and our liberty horses and ponies stood ready in the horse tent for the word to go into the ring. There is nothing like those moments just before the entry, when the *artistes* and all the other circus personnel, the animals included, are alert and keyed to what impends. And that is the way it was in the tents of the Cirkus Leopold in the early afternoon of that smiling summer day, at a moment of leashed and ready energies, when the sound of a drum came rolling with stentorian and practiced beat into the main tent: The police!

In Hungary, municipal and police department pronouncements were made by a town crier, who rolled a drum as an alert. So, when the drum rolled at our circus that day, all action ceased and ears were strained to hear. "Hear ye, hear ye, hear ye!" it came. "By order of the government of the municipality and the police department, a warning and an instruction to all persons! The Cirkus Leopold is by this order placed under quarantine!" The crier called out his message in the authoritatively projected voice of an adjutant issuing the orders of the day to a military formation, and our hearts sank as the information was imparted that an epidemic of the dreaded hoof and mouth disease had broken out in the vicinity, that the precincts of the circus were under quarantine and the premises were to be vacated at once by all persons not employed thereon. Our animals, all of them, were condemned to be delivered over to the authorities for destruction. Our tents, our costumes, and all articles made of cloth were to be seized and burned, and the personnel of the circus were to remain on the circus grounds until released.

Many eventful years have come and gone since that time,

and I was a mere boy when it happened, but I have never been able to forget the affliction of that hour, the sight of my sisters clinging to each other as they wept and cried out in agony when our horses were led away, and the anguished expression of my brother Sandor, who, being a man, had to take the blow in silence. For eight unhappy weeks we remained in that town, and for three or four of those weeks we were confined to the hot and dusty premises, having to get along with such provisions as the authorities brought us. When we were released at last from the quarantine and informed we were free to go, our predicament was like that of a legless man who has been told to arise and depart. Having no horses with which to haul our caravans, we first thought to rent the needed teams from villagers outside the zone of quarantine. But the owners of teams for hire were afraid of us and fled behind closed doors at our approach.

In the meantime, our money ran out and the provisions we had been able to buy were not enough to feed the 60 to 65 people in our company for more than a few days. My father, who was ill at this time of trial, could have borrowed the money we needed, but he was proud and feared debt. In these circumstances, therefore, we divided into small groups and in the manner of the wandering minstrels of the Middle Ages went out on foot into the towns and villages of the region and put on impromptu acts for such voluntary contributions as we could get. In this way, instead of resorting to robbery or theft, we put our talents to work and thus earned the money to buy bread. For weeks, drawing on our repertoire of proficiencies as acrobats, tumblers, dancers, and musicians, we presented our little acts, going to places that in some instances were as far away as 10 miles, until we had enough capital with which to buy a few horses and equipment. Later on we put together a variety show, working in halls, and, at length, were able to buy new tents and gradually to acquire new ring stock. We could not afford trained bareback horses, so we bought untrained horses and began making bareback horses out of them. In a liberty act the horses have to compose a uniform group, and it takes time to assemble them. When that has been accomplished, many months of training are required before a green group will work presentably at liberty. Faced with immediate financial needs, we could not delay long before showing again, so had to go back on the road with imperfectly trained bareback and liberty horses, going only to the villages and small towns until such time as our new stock could meet the requirements of a higher standard.

Severe ordeal though an experience like this was, it was the kind of thing to which circus people are accustomed and traditionally surmount. The mood of discouragement found no lodgement in our camp. We did the only thing we could do, and that was to work harder than ever. These efforts brought results, and, thus encouraged, we began aiming at new and higher goals, determined to bring a better Cirkus Leopold into being.

The Path of Our Bright Hopes and Progress

The illness of my father cast a shadow of concern across the path of our bright hopes and progress during the years that followed, imposing an added burden of responsibility on my mother. Nevertheless, under her direction, with my oldest brother, Sandor, at her right hand, our combined efforts in proprietorship and performance brought increasingly substantial rewards, and our troupe of bareback riders came on into the light of fame.

"Leopold Konyot is not a well man," said a gentleman from Szeged, "but his wife is an able woman, and it is she who now manages and directs the family circus. Mother Konyot comes by it naturally. She is a daughter of Simon Blumenfeld, of an old circus family, and there are those among us who remember her as a ballerina on the *panneau*,* one of the best. She may now indulge a mother's pride in the ladies and gentlemen who com-

* The *panneau* is the large, padded saddle of the ballerina on horseback.

pose the Konyot troupe of Hungarian riders. The Konyots are the parents of a dozen children, all of whom, even the youngest, are accomplished in the circus life."

We were all bareback riders, but were encouraged to develop additional skills, which accounts for the versatility in performance that served us so well as a circus-owning family. Sandor, my oldest brother, presented the liberty horses and worked as a clown. My other brothers and sisters had their own specialties. Adolph became accomplished as an acrobat and did a bar act. Both he and Gertrude were high-school riders and they made an act together. Max was a born animal trainer and a fine tumbler. In one of his animal acts of a few years later, 22 chimpanzees, dressed in a variety of costumes, danced together in ballroom style, lined up like a chorus in a musical review, and made up a band. Amalia was our best wire-walker. She was our best sewer also and had charge of making new costumes and repairing old ones. Amanda, Pepita, and Kathy had a flair for dancing and performed the *csardas, lassu* and *friss**, in native Hungarian costume. Alfons took to acrobatics like a duck to water, and Oscar, the youngest of the family, to his bareback riding as a matter of course. Olympia was already displaying the style and form that later made her one of the finest bareback equestriennes in the world. We all kept little Oscar busy, and out of mischief, more or less, running his legs off in the performance of errands. In recalling those days, he says he believes he knew more about what was going on in the circus than any of us, because he was in all parts of it so many times a day and every day in the week.

Both Adolph and I could usually be found in the horse tent when we were wanted somewhere else. It was by natural bent, in other words, that we became horse trainers. Adolph and I were *simpatico* and always worked together. My own first experience in the calling that was ultimately to become my

---

* The *csardas* is a national dance of Hungary and is characterized by its syncopated rhythms and contrasting tempos, i.e., *lassu*, or slow, and *friss*, which is fast and wild.

vocation was while I was in my early teens. I had begun to pester my mother for permission to try my hand at training some of our pony-sized horses and had begotten the admonition that the work I was doing in equestrian acrobatics was enough to keep me busy and that there would be time in the future for working with those little horses. Finally, when it became clear to her that I had set my heart on it, my mother relented and told me I could go ahead. I don't remember how long it took me, but the time came, to my own immense satisfaction, and the surprise, probably, of my parents, when I was able to put my little troop through a liberty drill routine with credit. I had learned how to go about it by watching my father, Sandor, and the great trainers in the Renz, Schumann, and Busch circuses. That is how one learns in the circus, by watching those who are masters.

Incidentally, in my opinion, the horse is one of the most difficult, if not the most difficult, of all animals to train, and this I say out of more than 50 years of experience as an animal trainer, in the course of which I have trained camels, elephants, bears, zebras, donkeys, monkeys, and dogs. The horse has a mind of his own. The dog, the seal, the camel, and the elephant will follow when the horse will not. They can be trained to follow on an open street or in an open area where there is nothing to confine them. The horse can be trained to follow, to be sure, but he will follow only when he is enclosed. The moment he sees he is not enclosed, he will be off on his own.

Some years ago there was a Mexican, by the name of Nelke, as I recall it, who had a high-schooled bull and a high-schooled camel, both of which made a change of leads, did a *pirouette* and a march, mounted a pedestal, bowed down, etc. I have trained camels at liberty myself. By camel I mean the two-humped Asiatic or Bactrian kind, which is preferred in the circus to the Arabian or Saharan single-humped camel, usually known as the dromedary.

II

The Famous Four Konyots

> Solo riding turns would be lost in the vast dimensions of a modern ring. The tendency is, therefore, to engage only equestrian groups, such as the Italian Casi Bisbinis or the Hungarian Konyots, eight or ten ladies and gentlemen, who finish their act by all jumping on the back of a single horse.
>
> —From CIRCUS NIGHTS AND CIRCUS DAYS, by
> Dr. A. H. Kober. Translated from the German by
> Claud W. Sykes.

We're Hired by Europe's Leading Circus Director

ONE FALL evening in 1903 in Vienna, just after we had presented our bareback act, a man came to the stables and introduced himself as Gerhard Gilgins of Berlin. He was an agent for the Zirkus Busch and the personal representative of Paul Busch, the manager and director. He had come to Vienna, he said, with a view of offering our bareback riders a contract to

11

present their act with the Zirkus Busch at its premiere in the German capital the following January. A conference with my parents was held, and after my mother had made the most of the sacrifice such an engagement would involve for our own circus, Herr Gilgins countered with such attractive terms that the matter was settled, and our star troupe, then consisting of Adolph, Max, Olympia, and myself, was signed up for the premiere, which was a gala event and a magnet of the entertainment world always. I was then 15 years old and had only recently become a member of the troupe.

The name of Busch loomed large in the firmanent of the European circus in those days. The long leading name of Renz had passed into history, but the example of the great Ernst Renz in establishing permanent circus buildings in such cities as Berlin, Vienna, Hamburg, and Breslau had been paralleled by Busch. Like their competitor, Albert Schumann, Sr., who had taken over the Renz interests, Paul Busch and his wife Constance, an equestrienne, continued pursuing the classical equestrian tradition and featuring the best horse acts money could hire. In his top hat, frock coat, and cape, with the waxed and upturned mustache of the period, Paul Busch personified the European circus director in the grand manner. That he was a perfectionist in his tastes and took pride in his reputation for approving of nothing but the best was well known. If he liked our act at the premiere, he would offer us a contract for an extended engagement. If he didn't like it, he would pay us off and we would be going home with an act that had been adjudged not good enough.

The six horses we took to Berlin were all Pinzgauers, an Austrian breed of heavy horses deriving its name from the district of Pinzgau in Styria, where it originated. Pinzgauers are usually roans and frequently have the spotted or splotched markings of what is known in this country as Appaloosa patterning over the quarters and flanks. Three of our horses were red roan appaloosas, two were blue roans, one a pinto, and all were good platforms and springboards for the jumping acrobatic riders. In short, because of their level way of going, their steadiness of pace, which comes from training and force of habit, and their unexcitable dispositions, they were made to order for such an act as ours. Turned out in silver-mounted black or white patent leather bridles, surcingles, and decorative breast-plates, they made a fine picture.

Upon our arrival in Berlin at the big stone building of the Zirkus Busch on Prasidenten Strasse, friends and strangers alike came forward with advice. One man, who was unknown to us, proffered the information that we were going to need applause to impress the great director, that it was the accepted practice to produce some pre-arranged hand-clapping, a claque, that is, and some well-timed bravos, for new acts at the premiere. It would be his pleasure, he said, to provide that commodity for us. There would be a charge, of course. To this suggestion we all responded with a complete lack of interest, Adolph replying that if the people liked our act they would applaud. We would try to make it good enough. From a trusted friend we learned that Commissionsrat* Busch was given to certain mannerisms that reliably indicated his reactions. If he was pleased with an act, he would lift his hat slightly and adjust it farther back on his head, and if displeased he would tilt it forward, place it well down on his brow, and assume an unmistakable expression.

Opening Night at the Zirkus Busch in Berlin

The minutes ticked off slowly during the last hour or so before opening time on that crucial and gala occasion, and the tension did not ease until the equestrian director blew his whistle, alerting all hands to be on the ready. From the dressing room, where we were getting into jockey uniforms, we could hear the concert music of the orchestra, which meant that the gate was open and the spectators were being ushered in. Precisely and on time, the

---

* Commissionsrat was a title given to citizens of the city of Berlin in recognition of notable achievement. The title was bestowed on both Paul Busch and his competitor, Albert Schumann, Sr.

animals of the circus, the elephants, the camels, the zebras, and a hundred or more horses, were being assembled and lined up for the parade that would open the show and display the opulence of one of the great circuses of the world. The *entrée* clowns now passed through the mounting room on their way into the ring. There was a flourish of trumpets, and the orchestra blared forth with the opening march. The premiere had begun.

As the time for our own entry drew near, our big, tried-and-true Pinzgauers, practice-perfect and inured to fanfare and bustle, stood calmly, while on the other side of the curtain, high above the tanbarked ring, four of the greatest aerialists in Europe were swinging to the music from their trapezes. Again came the sound of the whistle. This time it was for us. We sprang into the jockey saddles on our broad-backed mounts and cantered in single file into the ring.

A bareback act such as ours, with four or more riders, was divided into phases, of which there were, typically, four. Each phase was called a *reprise.* In our act the first *reprise* began with the four riders and four horses cantering around the ring in single file, the riders in their saddles. With the horses cantering, and always at an unvarying pace, the riders removed their saddles and assumed a standing position on the horses' rumps. The second *reprise* began with the withdrawal of two of the horses and the performance of acrobatics, the four riders working with the two remaining horses, two riders to each horse. The third *reprise* began with a demonstration of simultaneous jumping, the riders on each of the two horses jumping at the same time from the horse to the ground and back again, and from horse to horse, and ended with all four riders jumping in unison from the ground to the backs of the two horses. In the fourth *reprise,* which was the finale, one of the two horses was withdrawn, the bridle, surcingle, and breastplate were removed from the single remaining horse, and the four riders jumped on and off the one horse, in succession, one, two, three, and four, and back again simultaneously, with the horse at a gallop. There were variations in this routine, of course, and it was normal to make pyramids and a *pas-de-deux*.

From the vantage point of his box, which overlooked the ring, Commissionsrat Busch kept a monocled eye on the performance. By the time we had completed the second *reprise* his top hat was still in place. As we began the fourth, the finale, he adjusted it farther back on his head, which indicated approval, if our friend was to be believed. A few minutes after we had returned to the stable, following the act, he appeared before us wearing a smile and, after congratulating us, proceeded to book us for an extended engagement—six months more in Berlin, two in Hamburg, two in Breslau, and two in Vienna.

I Watch a Great High-School Rider Train

That night at the premiere I saw Burckhardt-Footit ride. A former juggler on horseback, and an artist of the saddle, who, like Petoletti, Kisner, Albert Schumann, Mathilde Monnet, and Theresa Renz, followed in the footsteps of the masters, Burckhardt-Footit was the equestrian director of the Zirkus Busch. He was the husband, moreover, of Paula Busch, the daughter of Paul and Constance Busch, and it was he, or so it has been said, who was responsible for the fabulous water pantomimes and equestrian pageants of that justly famous circus. Noted for his excellence of position and an instinctive artistry as an exhibitionist, he made a fine equestrian figure in top hat and the formal attire of the European riding ring. It was after having seen him ride that my own ambitions took a serious turn in the direction of high-school exhibition.

Burckhardt-Footit had a ring of his own at the Zirkus Busch, in which he worked his horses in the early morning. From this ring all others were excluded, and no spectators were allowed. I managed to find a way into this sanctum, however, and from a position where I hoped I would not be detected watched the master working and exercising his horses in the various stages of their schooling.

One day he discovered me and brought me up short, demanding to know who I was and what I was about. When he came closer and recognized me as one of the Konyots, he softened and, after I had told him of my admiration and desire only to learn, gave me permission to watch him in his work, which I continued to do at every opportunity over the ensuing months. This led to his becoming interested enough in me to often explain what he was doing, and why, and to give me actual instructions. In addition to training his own horses, Burckhardt-Footit trained a few horses for others. He also trained the riders, one of whom was Martha Mohnke, who rode the side saddle and held the reins in her left hand.

Four Years in 'The Big Time'

Toward the end of our first year in the Zirkus Busch we signed up for an engagement of six months in the Cirkus Beketow, which began in Budapest.

Matthias Beketow, a Russian by birth and a Hungarian by adoption, was an able circus director who had begun his career as a clown with a trained pig. His Cirkus Beketow was known for the excellence of its equestrian acts. Henrico Gautier, the equestrian director, trained and presented the liberty horses and rode the high-school.

We went on a tour of Europe and the Balkans in the Cirkus Beketow the following spring, showing in Paris, Copenhagen, Belgrade, and Bucharest, with stops at innumerable places along the route. During this tour my sister Gertrude and my brother Alfons joined our bareback troupe, which now consisted of six riders, and we were billed henceforth as "The Famous Six Konyots."

On returning to the Zirkus Busch for another year, we had an act that was more outstanding than ever, and began to present it in formal attire—Adolph, Max, Alfons, and I in full dress, the girls in evening gowns.

Ill fortune, forever lurking in the shadows of the circus world, entered at this stage to dog our steps. Adolph fell ill and

couldn't work. Max injured a knee and went to the hospital, and
Alfons followed him there a few days later with a dislocated
ankle. This left only three of us to carry on. Then, within less
than a month, Gertrude broke her ankle, leaving only Olympia
and me to work together.

At this time, Commissionsrat Busch, exacting taskmaster
though he was, gave proof of his considerateness. The recupera-
tive powers of youth did the rest, and in less time than might
have been expected all six Konyots were working again and
doing their best to retrieve the lost time. A return engagement
of six months in th Cirkus Beketow and another six months in
Hengler's Circus in England, which was under Matthias Beketow's direction for that time and included a Christmas Show at
Olympia in London, brought us into 1908.

We had been away for four years. My parents thought that
was long enough, so they summoned us back to the family circus
in Budapest.

Parties, Pranks and Merriment in the Circus

Life in the circus was not all work and striving. Togetherness,
nurtured by mutuality in the trials and rewards of an under-
taking in common, found ready expression in the lighter vein.
We had numerous parties after the show in celebration of birth-
days and anniversaries, of which there was a steady flow, and
it was on these occasions that the hard-working people of the
circus found release from their labors in merriment and fun-
making. Of musical talent, both as regards the playing of instruments and singing, there was no lack. And when there was
music, there was dancing, for which a wooden platform was laid
down in the ring. Everyone contributed, in one way or another,
to the entertainment at these usually impromptu affairs, and if,
at times, the gayety reached hilarious proportions, that came
about in natural release and not through indulgence in alcohol.
For the code of conduct was strong, and the misuse and abuse
of intoxicants was frowned upon.

Of our home life in the Cirkus Leopold, especially as of the
last years of it, just prior to the first World War, I have vivid
and happy memories. By that time my older brothers and
sisters were married and their wives and husbands had become
members of our large family group, which added up to 27
people, four or five of them grandchildren. We had our meals
together and almost always had guests, so that there were sel-
dom fewer than 30 people at the family table. Despite the burden of managing a circus and ministering to my father, who had
become a semi-invalid, my mother was a devoted and efficient
home-maker and a cook of some fame. As the products of her
training, my sisters were all accomplished in the domestic arts,
and, together with my sisters-in-law, did the house-cleaning in
our living wagons and the dish-washing in the cook-house, and
helped my mother with the cooking.

Neither my father nor my mother was particularly musical,
but, Max and I excepted, their children were. Sandor was an
accomplished flutist and played the trumpet well. Adolph and
Alfons both played the violin and guitar, and Amalia's husband,
Henry Kittel, was a pianist and guitarist of considerable ability,
Olympia played the concertina and the guitar, and Adolph's
wife, Lilly, the concertina and mandolin. The nearest I ever
came to being a musician was as a drummer, in which humble
capacity I could at least follow the tempo of the music. Ex-
posed, as I was, however, to good music, I did develop an ear
for it and a sense of rhythm, which is essential to the bareback
rider and the rider of high-school horses.

There is a lively sense of humor among circus people, and
one of the ways in which this finds expression is in good natured
practical joking. I recall, for example, a joke that was played on
me back in the 1920's while we were in France in the Cirque
Napoleon Rancy.

On the morning of a bright summer day in one of the provincial cities along the route, two of my fellow *artistes* and I were
out shopping. Presently, we came to a shoe store and stopped to
look in the show window.

"Now there is a pair of shoes that I could use," said one of my two companions. "They look like a bargain. Let's go in." We did, and we each bought a pair of shoes. My friends bought white and black ones, respectively, and I settled for a brown pair. A few days later, the man who bought the white shoes came to me and said, "Arthur, these white shoes don't fit me. Since I can't go back to exchange them, I'll let you have them for half price, if they fit you. Try them on." I tried them on, and, *mirabile dictu,* they fitted me perfectly, so I bought them.

After a few minutes, I walked over to my wagon to put my new purchase in the shoe compartment of my trunk, only to discover that the brown shoes I had bought previously were missing. At that moment, as I puzzled over the matter, I heard some chuckling, and when I found, on looking up, that it was coming from my two shopping companions of a few days before, I tumbled. My friends had taken the brown shoes out of my trunk, very neatly painted them white, and sold them back to me.

"Here, Arthur," said the culprit, as he handed my money back to me. "Now you have a fine pair of new white shoes." I bowed in acknowledgement, and all three of us laughed heartily.

Of all the circus proprietors I have known, Napoleon Rancy takes the palm as the most original and habitual practical joker. As an example of the kind of prank he used to be up to, I recall a night on the road when the *artistes* all found their shoes missing after the show. There were a lot of tired people running around the circus grounds in their stocking feet or bare-footed that night, and they were just about ready to give up the search when someone discovered the missing shoes. They had been run aloft on the center poles of the tents—the shoes of the entire personnel—and were visible there in the moonlight! It was Napoleon Rancy who had conceived the idea and ordered the job done.

On another occasion Napoleon Rancy's son Henri was the victim of circus humor—not of one of his father's practical jokes but at the hands of fellow *artistes.* This was after Henri had begun to ride the high-school and just after he had equipped himself with a new formal riding habit and a new silk top hat for his act. One night, upon emerging from his wagon, with his act about to come up, he began sniffing the air with a pained expression. There was a bad smell. Others noted the unpleasantness, too, as Henri approached them—and even more so as he came into their close company. That there was something rotten in the circus was distressingly certain, and to Henri the indication of the foulness seemed all-pervading. Presently the thought came to him, to his horror, no doubt, that the cause of the sadness might be on his own person. However, it was too late to do anything about it, because the time to mount his horse was at hand and he was being called up.

The discomfort of the poor man can be imagined, as he sat in the saddle preparatory to entering the ring, with everyone about him holding his nose, and, as he made his act, with the stench adhering to him or pursuing him, the people at ringside also holding their noses, as he passed by. In the privacy of his wagon, to which he had retreated in disconsolate haste, after his act, he found the source of the offensiveness. A practical joker had procured a ribbon of one of the foulest smelling cheeses on the face of the earth and inserted it neatly under the hat band of his black topper.

III

A Deal with John Ringling

Hungary is the home of the Konyots, who are the famous family known the world over as artistes and directors. Professionally, they are known as *the Four Konyot Brothers,* but their clan appears to be as large as that of the Blumenfelds, for Sandor Konyot, who now superintends the erection of their big tent, has confessed to five brothers and six sisters, all of whom are circus folk.

> —From CIRCUS NIGHTS AND CIRCUS DAYS, by
> Dr. A. H. Kober. Translated from the German by
> Claud W. Sykes.

We Go to America

IN 1907, a year after the death of James A. Bailey, the Ringling Brothers acquired the Barnum & Bailey Circus, and in 1908, while in Europe in search of talent and new acts, John Ringling, next to the youngest of the seven brothers,* came to Vienna to

* Albert C. (1852-1916), August (1854-1907), Otto (1858-1911), Alfred T. (1861-1919), Charles (1863-1926), John (1866-1936), Henry (1869-1918).

21

see our bareback act. The name of Ringling was already famous in Europe, and I remember how electrified we were one day, while at luncheon in the cook house, when my mother told us she had just had a telephone call from John Ringling of the celebrated Ringling brothers, and that Mr. Ringling was coming to Vienna on the morrow. We all surmised, of course, what the great American circus magnate probably had in mind and were thrilled with the thought that a trip to America might be in store for us, although my parents seemed less enthusiastic over such a possibility. The next evening, after our bareback act, Mr. John, as he was known in the circus, came to the stable, spoke well of our performance, and introduced himself. Later that evening he had a conference with my parents, at which I was present, and I can still hear my mother saying "no" to Mr. John's statement that he wanted to book our bareback troupe for an engagement with the newly acquired Barnum & Bailey Circus.

"These children of ours have been everywhere but here in our own circus for four years and they only recently came back," she said. "Mr. Konyot's health has not been improving and we cannot get along without them."

My mother was a good business woman and when she saw that Mr. John was not going to be easily dissuaded, she said to him, "If you must have the troupe, Mr. Ringling, you will have to take the rest of us along with them, and we are a lot of people."

"And how many is that?" Mr. John queried.

"Well," said my mother, "there are more than 20 of us. With our two daughters-in-law, four sons-in-law, and two grandchildren, there are 22. However, we have a faithful servant, a woman who has been with us for many years, who will have to be included. That makes 23. We will have to take two grooms, so that makes 25."

Mr. John smiled, and knowing that we were all people of the circus, settled for 25, saying that he would find something for most of our large group to do. It was agreed that, in addition to eight bareback horses, we were to bring two high-school horses and the liberty horses Bella and Pantolan, but my father interjected with the statement that he would sign no contract that did not include his three old pensioners, Emir, Satan and Lucifer. Under no circumstances, he said, would he be willing to leave them at home in the care of grooms. They, too, would have to go to America. Mr. John smiled again, and looking directly at my father, said, "Mr. Konyot, I want you to be happy, too. I sympathize with you in the feeling you have for your old horses. Bring them along."

With no further obstacles remaining, terms were agreed upon and a contract was signed that night. The contract was for two years at $500 a week, with all traveling expenses to the United States for 25 people, all living expenses for the duration of the contract, including the use of a large house in Bridgeport, Conn., during the winter months, to be assumed by the Ringlings. Beyond that, Mr. John gave his personal assurance that the members of our family group, other than those who composed the bareback troupe, would be paid additionally at going rates for such work as the management assigned to them, and, as was well known, John Ringling's word was as good as gold.

Sailing from Hamburg late in the winter of 1909, we made the crossing on the Hamburg-American steamship *Graf Waldersee* to Hoboken, N.J., and from Hoboken went directly to the Barnum & Bailey winter quarters in Bridgeport, where we placed ourselves at the disposal of the management and began making ready for the opening of the season of 1909 in Chicago.

It took four long trains to transport the huge Barnum & Bailey Circus, which was now owned and managed by the Ringlings, but continued to proclaim itself "The Greatest Show On Earth" and cited its composition in the following figures in support of that claim: 1,280 persons; 700 horses; 400 performers; 100 acts, features, and sensations; 40 elephants; 30 camels; 60 great riders; 60 aerialists; 50 clowns; 60 acrobats; 60 gymnasts and 6 arenas, including "the biggest tent ever made, 540 feet long, seating 15,000 people, with a ¼-mile hippodrome track."

Four long trains, with a total of 85 double length cars! On one of those trains was our own little company of 25 people, which consisted of my brothers Sandor, Adolph, Max, Alfons, and Oscar; my sisters Amalia, Amanda, Kathy, Pepita, Olympia, and Gertrude; Sandor's wife Helen Deike, Max's wife Anna Milatz, Amalia's husband Henry Kittel, Amanda's husband Tony Webb, Kathy's husband Anton Pilch, Adolph's fiance Lilly Reinsch, Kathy's two children, my mother and father, our old servant, two grooms, and myself.

'The Greatest Show on Earth'

The Six Konyots. First Time Here Of The Great Magyar Riding Troupe. Dashing Feats Of Whirlwind Jockey Carrying, Jumping & Acrobatic Equitation. An Entirely New Act.

—From a BARNUM & BAILEY PROGRAM, 1909.

From the opening performance in Chicago's Coliseum in the spring of 1909 to the conclusion of our engagement three years later, our bareback troupe was assigned to the center ring, the top spot. "The Riding Davenports" and the team of Fred Derrick, a great English acrobatic rider, and Ella Bradna worked in the rings to the right and left of us. Orin Davenport, an all-time great among the acrobatic riders, his wife Victoria and sister May had no peer among the troupes of that day. Ella Bradna was the wife of Fred Bradna, equestrian director of the Barnum & Bailey Circus, and had been a featured star for a number of years. In his book *The Big Top* (New York, 1952), recalling the years in which the Konyots were with the Barnum & Bailey Circus, the late Fred Bradna states (page 90), "The Konyots, whom I hired in Europe, were all over the program, six times appearing by name and five times as Spelvins, the name traditionally utilized to cover duplication in castings." He is mistaken in his recollection of having hired us, for, as I have already said, it was John Ringling himself who did so. He is not mistaken about our having been "all over the program." Mr.

John, it will be remembered, had told my mother in Vienna that he would find something for most of our large family group to do. A summation of our activities makes clear that he did.

Sandor's wife, Helen Deike, of a famous family of acrobats and wire-walkers, did a wire act. So did my sister Amalia, under the name of Mlle. Lipot. Adolph and Gertrude rode the high-school in duo on the track, as well as in company with a group of "lady and gentlemen leaders of *Haute École*," as they were referred to in the program. Lilly and I did a *pas de deux*, in which the man, standing astride two horses, holds the reins in one hand while swinging his lady partner into various positions with the other, the lady assuming graceful poses, standing on the man's shoulders, etc. The *pas de deux* is in the tradition of the classical circus.

The Barnum & Bailey Circus was especially strong in elephant acts, and the performances in all three rings were invariably excellent. Featured were "The Rossie Musical Elephants," in which the elephants shook bells of different tonalities and made other musical sounds by sliding their trunks up and down tubes or pipes. The production of these sounds was facilitated by the application of resin to the trunks, which increased the friction. Amanda, Pepita, Olympia, and Gertrude rode the Rossie titans and gave a demonstration of acrobatics on their backs. That was in 1909.

Harry J. Mooney's "Musical Elephant Prodigies" were a center ring attraction in 1910. These elephants blew horns and from sitting postures beat drums and played violas, moving enormous bows back and forth over the strings with their trunks.

For the circus of 1910 Adolph and I trained 24 horses in a three-ring tandem act, eight horses and four riders performing in each of the three rings. Riding one horse, each rider drove an unmounted horse in long reins in front of him, the four riders in each ring working as a unit in the execution of a variety of tandem maneuvers. The horses were all Appaloosas, or "leopard" horses, in European parlance. Two of the four riders in each ring were women, and my sisters Olympia and Gertrude were among them.

As all this illustrates, Bradna did not indulge in overstatement when he recalled that the Konyots were "all over the program." There was still more that we did. As "The Three Bokromas," Adolph's wife Lilly, Amanda's husband Tony Webb, and I worked in the center ring in a combined juggling act on horseback. Tony was one of the greatest jugglers on horseback. We juggled balls, plates, fire, and rings while balancing on the backs of the galloping horses. Three of our family group, Sandor, Henry Kittel, and Anton Pilch, worked as clowns. Henry was a former acrobat and strong man, while Anton had been a circus manager and director.

And, finally, we trained "The Great Balloon Horse Jupiter," as he was called, to stand motionless on a platform secured to a balloon, the horse maintaining his position without moving as the balloon and the platform with it were drawn upward by a masked pulley mechanism. Fireworks were then set off along the perimeter of the platform, the horse continuing to hold his pose as the fireworks went off on all sides of him and the whole contraption descended. The illusion, of course, was that the platform, with the horse and his lady rider on it, were being borne aloft by the balloon. The act was publicized as "A Sensational Ascension Act, With A Gorgeous Pyrotechnic Display, Barnum & Bailey's Latest And Greatest Thriller."

Fred Bradna was in error also in the matter of dates. He reported that it was in 1913 that we were contracted, but in 1913 we were back on the other side of the Atlantic, after having spent three years in this country, and we were going full blast as performers and as the proprietors of our own circus.

"After 1914," writes Bradna in *The Big Top* (page 57), "the Konyots, a Hungarian equestrian family, always came down at this time from the circus winter quarters in Bridgeport to play the violin, mandolin, flute and zither. There was dancing in the front parlor." Again the date is wrong. I remember those occasions. But that all took place in 1909, 1910, and 1911.

On Tour with Barnum & Bailey

Most of our stands during the summer-long tours, which covered thousands of miles in the United States and Canada, were for one and two days, so that the personnel spent many, if not most, of the nights in the Pullmans. Those were the days of the great street parades, which went out at 10 o'clock in the morning, rain or shine, and in which everyone had to take part. The members of our troupe and others of the family group rode horseback, using horses from the circus ring stock, which were accustomed to the crowds and the hubbub on the city streets. Decked out in ornate and richly colored costumes provided by the management, we sometimes rode in the *howdahs* on the backs of the elephants, in carriages, or on floats. A feature of the Barnum & Bailey street parades was the enormous red band wagon, embellished with gold leaf carvings, and drawn by 40 red-plumed Percherons, which were harnessed in 10 rows, four to the row. Another was the steam calliope at the end of the procession, a huge, piping contraption, also red and gold, which could be heard from afar. It took an hour for the whole mammoth parade to pass, which suggests the reason why the wonderful circus parades of yesterday have gone the way of the dinosaur.

The life of a trouper while on tour in the Barnum & Bailey Circus was strenuous. The day began, typically, after a night on the Pullman, with an early morning arrival at a new destination. The men whose function was to load and unload the cars, the razorbacks, in American circus parlance, lost no time in transferring everything from the cars to the wagons and hauling it from the railroad siding to the circus grounds. The hauling of the animal cages and the heavy equipment was done with teams, fours, and even multiple hitches of powerful draft horses. Elephants did some of the heaviest work, such as shunting the cars into position for loading and unloading and pulling the ropes that raise the "big top," and they stood ready to perform the not infrequently necessary task of extricating the wagons from a bog-down after heavy rains.

The area of the circus grounds became the scene of a remarkably well-organized operation on these arrivals, as the gangs of "big top" men, under the direction of the tent masters, applied their know-how to an agglomeration of canvas, masts, pulleys, guy-ropes, wooden forms, and iron anchors, wherewith the tented city of "The Greatest Show on Earth" came miraculously into being. After the trunks had been unpacked, breakfast, which was almost a ritual, was served in the cookhouse, and after breakfast one had to begin making ready for the street parade.

Thereafter, it was time for lunch, following which preparations for the matinee had to be under way. When the matinee was over, with supper soon to come up, there was a brief period during which one could be at leisure. Supper was light, and after it all action was pointed toward the evening performance, the climax of nearly every passing day, which began at 8:15 and was not over until 11:00. On the conclusion of the evening performance, every night after one-day stands and every other night after two-day stands, which was most of the time, the operation of dismantling the circus was in order. Actually, the dismantling was begun while the show was still going on, and in a surprisingly short time after the crowds had gone the canvas dome of the "big top" came down. With the same dispatch that had described its erection, the tented city vanished from the precincts, which were left in quietude to commune with the stars.

Despite the relentless regimen governing one's life while on tour in such an organization, get-togethers and parties were of regular occurrence after the shows during the longer stands. Performers eat sparingly before the show and are ready for a feast afterward. Adolph's widow, Lilly, who now lives in Sarasota, recalls how Fred Bradna, Eddie Siegrist, and young Alfredo Codona used to come around after the performance to partake of her own and the Konyots' Hungarian dishes, her *bala chinkin,* for example. Happy occasions, those, at which the gang got together to make a fire, around it to sing, enjoy good food, and make merry. Sharing was the keynote to the happiness, the sharing of food, fun, music, song, and troubles. The members of our family group were always ready with their musical instruments and repertoire of old-world melodies, which included the gypsy music of Hungary, ever a favorite. Those were the days of rag-time and of popular songs that somehow expressed the mood and spirit of the more exuberant and carefree U.S.A. of that time. The instrumentalists in our family group learned to play American tunes with a lilt and flair, and nationality was no bar to singing "Oh, You Beautiful Doll," "Everybody's Doing It," "By the Light of the Silvery Moon," "Every Little Movement," etc.

It was the custom of the Ringlings to give a party for the circus personnel on Saturday nights after the show. These affairs were held in a hotel, always one of the best in town. Food and refreshments to please the most discriminating were served. There was music, there was dancing, and everyone had fun. Alfred Ringling, Otto, and John were in charge of the Barnum & Bailey unit, and if all three of them were not always at the parties, one or two of them invariably were. Mingling freely among the people of the circus, they entered into the merriment and seemed to enjoy themselves equally with the rest.

The Saturday night parties were an illustration of the active interest the Ringlings took in the morale of the people who worked for them. The brothers saw to it that only the best food was served in the cookhouse; they had their own meals there and partook of the same fare. Since the circus personnel in those days had reason to feel that their efforts were being appreciated, there was a fine *esprit de corps.* Everyone did his or her best.

There were more than a few big names among the hundreds of performers on the Barnum & Bailey programs of 1909, 1910, and 1911. In 1910 Alfredo Codona, then only 16, and later to win recognition as the unmatched flyer of all time, made a single, swinging trapeze act that was sensational. His sister

Victoria performed on the slack wire. Among the aerialists, in addition to Codona, there were such troupes as the Siegrist-Silbon Troupe of 15, the Charles Siegrist Troupe, the "Flying LaMars," and the English team of Charles and Ernest Clarke. These performances were matched in acrobatics by the acts of the Julius Dollar, American Florence, Picciani, Pati Frank, and Grunathos troupes, the latter of women, and the Seresto Sisters. Lillian Leitzel, the tiny and incomparable aerial gymnast from Breslau, Germany, was on the program in 1911 as one of the "Four Leamy Ladies," the others being her mother and two of her mother's sisters. Leitzel, whose real name was Lillian Alize Elianore, was then 18 and had just come over from Germany. Best remembered among the clowns are Adolph Oshansky, long a favorite in the American circus, and the then white-faced clown Pat Valdo, originally a juggler and wire walker, who later became the widely known and beloved ringmaster and director of personnel of the combined Ringling Brothers and Barnum & Bailey Circus.

After the season of 1909 Max and his wife returned to Europe, leaving us with three men and two women in our bareback troupe. It was then that we brought young Oscar, who was only 12, into the act and dressed him up as a girl, so as to make a troupe of three men and three women. Oscar, who had taken so to "cowboying", writhed in displeasure at the sight of his wig and the costume that went with it. However, he made a very acceptable girl and found an impish sort of pleasure in the role. There were so many Konyots that people were not surprised at the appearance of another one, and for a time thought that the new little bareback rider was the sister of the boy who was such a familiar sight in cowboy garb all over the circus every day. The boy was a bareback rider, too, they averred. They had seen him in rehearsal and he was just as good as his sister, though they liked her best.

During the season of 1910 Adolph was kicked by one of the circus horses and suffered a compound fracture of the shin bone. He was sent to Bridgeport to recuperate and had to be laid off for the season. Despite that long absence, his salary was not cut for a single day, which again illustrated the attitude of the Ringlings toward their people. As a result of his injury, Adolph had a slight limp for the rest of his life, but continued to be the fine bareback rider he had always been. He and Lilly Reinsch, who came to the United States with us as one of our family group, were married in 1910 in Bridgeport. Lilly was a Kolzer on her mother's side, and the Kolzers, like the Reinsch family, were of old circus tradition.

There were two blow-downs in the Barnum & Bailey Circus during our 1909-1911 engagement, and the one I remember best was the blow-down of the tent, half of which served as the stable for the performing horses and the other half as the dressing room. The ground was soggy from heavy rains, and a wind of near-gale force pulled the stakes, whereupon the tent began to move against the ties with the wind. This was perilous, of course, because it threatened to bring the heavy tent poles crashing down with the tent itself on top of the horses. There was only one thing to do under the circumstances, and it had to be done at once: Take the tent down from the inside at the center.

The canvas would have to lie on the horses for a few minutes, and there was risk in that. The whole thing was done with finesse, however. The canvas was then sliced into sections and moved, piecemeal, from over the horses. The horsemen stayed with their charges and kept them quiet.

Upon the expiration of our two-year contract, John Ringling proposed a renewal, but my parents were getting homesick and would sign for only one more year, which would take us through 1911.

"No, Mr. Ringling," said my father to the proposal. "As you know, I am not well. Two years is a long time. I may be dead by then, and I prefer to die in my own country."

We went back to Europe in 1912 with some new ideas, impatience to put them into effect, and a bulging purse. In addition to what we were paid under the contract for our center-ring bareback act, we were well paid for our other activities, and were free to accept bookings for performances in our various capacities in the vaudeville theatres during the winter. Our earnings were, therefore, sizeable.

We Konyots of the bareback troupe were forerunners of such star troupes as those of the Hanafords, the Repinski family, and the talented and versatile Cristiani family of the present day.

Because of extremes of climate and the effects of being quartered for so much of the time in the cars, a number of the horses we brought with us from Europe in 1909 did not survive their three years in the United States. An enduring survivor was Sigi, the priceless 17-hand Pinzgauer we all jumped on to simultaneously in the finale of the bareback act. Toward the end of the season of 1909 Sigi went lame and couldn't work. The services of the circus veterinarians combined with our own best efforts at doctoring were getting nowhere, so John Ringling called in a noted Bridgeport veterinarian by the name of Sutton and made a proposition to him, saying:

"If you succeed in making this horse go sound, so that he can work again, as before, in addition to paying your bill for services, I will buy you a complete new outfit of clothes: a suit, overcoat, hat, shoes, socks, shirt, necktie and everything else, the finest money will buy."

Dr. Sutton, applying himself with great energy and thoroughness, found that Sigi had broken a small bone in one of his front legs, so he operated on him and visited him nearly every day thereafter. In two months the horse was sound again, and we returned him gradually to work. Dr. Sutton got his new clothes and a box of the best Havana cigars to boot.

IV

The End of an Era

The Konyot Circus and Wild West Show

ON OUR RETURN to Europe in 1912, we established headquarters at Mahrisch-Ostrau, in what was then the Austrian crownland of Moravia, and there put together a circus, added a new feature to it and called it "The Konyot Brothers Great American Circus & Wild West Show."

We got the idea of the Wild West feature from the Buffalo Bill, Pawnee Bill, and Miller Brothers 101 Ranch Shows, which we saw during our three years in the United States, and began laying plans for it while on tour in the Barnum & Bailey Circus. Borrowing from the authentic American versions, we had all the standard features: the robbery of the stagecoach by masked outlaws, the attack by mounted Indians on the prairie schooners, and demonstrations of trick-roping and sharpshooting. We brought no redskins back with us from the United States, but we

did bring back a lot of cowboy equipment and a quantity of
feathered head-dresses, beaded vests, and moccasins, and with
this paraphernalia made cowboys, American style, out of Hungarians, and Indians out of Algerians and other people with
copper-colored skins. Our "Indians" looked the part and rode
with all the war-whooping abandon of a party of Sioux. An
American might not have been convinced, but our European
audiences were thrilled. Even more thrilled was Oscar, who
could now be a cowboy in earnest, and proved himself expert
with the lasso and lariat. So well received was our new enterprise that we were soon able to augment our ring stock with
many new animals and to replace our old caravans with the
finest money could buy. We were riding the crest of the wave
in successful showmanship and dreaming of new worlds to
conquer.

In January, 1914, the Konyot Brothers Great American Circus
& Wild West Show went into winter quarters in the home city
of Budapest and began making preparations for the next season's tour, to begin in the spring. That same month my mother
died. Who, better than we, could have realized the measure of
our loss, unless it was my father, who had been an invalid for
so long and expected to precede my mother in death? It was
my mother, more than anyone, we owed our success to, both
in performance and as circus proprietors. It was she who for
many years had directed our efforts, fired our ambitions and
kept our sights high.

I Meet Manya Guttenberg

One evening in March, 1914, I saw a beautiful ballerina in a
performance in the Cirkus Barogaldi and knew my life could
never be the same again. Her name was Manya Guttenberg.
Manya, her two brothers, and Boggy Yelding* of the English
circus family composed the Guttenberg Reiterei of that day,
and Manya was the star of the troupe. Manya was born in Vladi-

* My sister Gertrude later married Boggy Yelding and became a British citizen.

Olympia Konyot in 1908.

Amalia (Konyot) Kittel.

Amanda (Konyot) Webb.

Adolph Konyot.

My parents, Leopold and Henrietta Konyot.

Max Konyot.

THE ACKNOWLEDGED LEADERS IN STARTLING AND BEAUTIFUL CREATIONS OF THE EQUESTRIAN ART.

NEW ACTS OF PERIL AND FASCINATION NEVER SEEN BEFORE.

THE KÖNYÖT FAMILY OF SIX STARTLING SENSATIONAL HUNGARIAN RIDERS,
NEVER BEFORE SEEN OUTSIDE THEIR NATIVE LAND.

Program frontispiece for Barnum & Bailey Circus, 1909.

High spirits in the Barnum & Bailey Circus. My brother Adolph balances on my
shoulders, at right; others in this hitherto unpublished photograph are the acrobat
Julius Dollar, third from left; Joe de Cooke of the great Joe & Tony de Cooke
equilibrist team, second from left, and my brother Max, to right of cannon,
wearing cap.

"The Six Konyots: Hungarian Riders," as we appeared with Barnum & Bailey, 1911. Left to right: Arthur, Olympia, Alfons, Oscar (in girl's costume), Adolph and Gertrude. Standing, Sandor.

Arthur Konyot in 1911.

Adolph's wife Lily and I, as we appeared in a *pas-de-deux* act.

My brother Alfons.

Dressed up for our Wild West Show,
Budapest, 1913.

Our version of a Wild West troupe—the Konyot Brothers Great American Circus
on tour in Europe in 1913.

My brother Sandor.

My sister Kathe (Konyot) Pilch.

Manya Guttenberg, my future wife, as she appeared when I first met her in 1914.

This picture, taken in 1922, when we were in Paris with the Nouveau Cirque, shows our bareback troupe as a musical sextette.

In the Cirque Rancy in 1925 I was engaged to instruct Napoleon Rancy's son Henri (right) in high-school riding. In this picture, made at Bordeaux, France, my mount is the 32-year-old Ace, a great old high-school horse trained by Albert Schumann, Sr.

Topsy, Darling, Jim and Teddy, the stars of my bear act in Portugal. My Siberian friends were getting big, but they were not yet full-grown.

A solo bareback act with my faithful old Boyar in Spain.

Boyar and Romeo with grooms.

Pinto Silgo (left) and Nobre in rehearsal in France. Trained for combat in the Portuguese bull ring, they excelled as high-school horses and performed as a pair in a liberty act.

Free shoulder action in high degree—Manya and Sultan in Portugal. I never saw another horse with such action. (See below.)

Manya as a bareback equestrienne.

Seeing is believing. Here is photographic proof. I am the rider this time.

A moment of leisure at our home on wheels somewhere in Europe in the early 1930's. Standing, left to right: Arthur Herman Althoff of the German circus family, my son Alexander and my daughter Dorita. Seated, left to right: Dora Althoff, Frau Schirmer, Manya and the daughter and granddaughter of Frau Schirmer.

Manya and Vulcan somewhere in Europe. Vulcan is doing a Spanish trot.

Poster advertising our high-school act with the Cirque d' Hiver.

Manya and I as we appeared in our serio-comic bareback act, "Miss Marietta."

My brother Adolph and Canario, the splendid Andalusian horse I bought in the Azores.

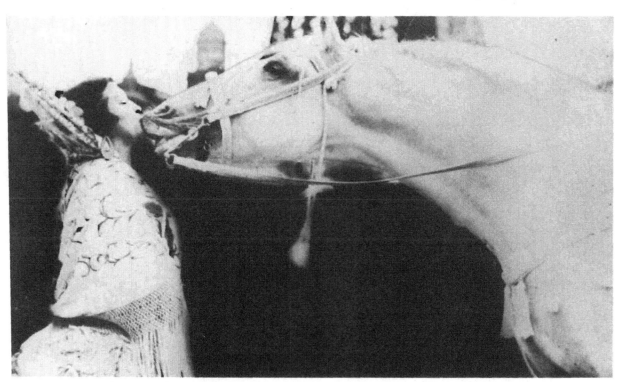

The fiery and beautiful Vulcan worked for Manya as he would for no one else.

Here we are in the ring.

Training an octette of Percherons for a liberty act at the Ringling Brothers and
Barnum & Bailey Circus winter quarters at Sarasota, Fla., in 1942.

My daughter Dorita and the Russian Orloff Kaitan.

Training Colonel Washington, an American saddle horse, Sarasota, Fla.

Dorita and Nobre do the canter on three legs, Ringling Brothers and Barnum & Bailey, 1941.

A good picture of rearing horses. My daughter Dorita is at left astride Luzero.
Her companion is Estelle Butler, a pupil of mine, on Kaitan.

Here Colonel Washington is doing the *passage*. The Colonel was one of the best high-school horses I ever owned.

When my son Alexander came back from the war in 1946, he joined Dorita and me to work as a threesome in Orin Davenport's Shrine Circus.

Ready for the act. Dorita and her high-school horse Bomba on the road with
Orin Davenport's Shrine Circus.

kavkaz, Russia, and was then 23. Her mother, Irene Pavlova Guttenberg, a second cousin of Anna Pavlova, famed of the Russian ballet, had been adopted as a child by her aunt. Her aunt had married into the Truzzi family, equestrians and directors in the Russian circus, though they were of Italian origin. So Manya's mother, Irene, grew up in an environment of equestrianism and show business, to become a ballerina on the *panneau* and a *parforce* rider. Father Guttenberg, a former acrobat, was an exemplar of the classical in presentation and performance, and the Guttenberg Reiterei were the product of his tutelage, as well as of the Pavlova-Truzzi traditions.

After seeing Manya that evening in the Cirkus Barogaldi, my work as a bareback rider became of secondary importance. Life in the circus was confining, but I took advantage of every opportunity to invite her to go with me for refreshments to a restaurant in the Varosliget, Budapest's famous municipal park, where there was an especially fine cymbalom* and violin orchestra. The musicians, all of them gypsies, came to know us well, and one of the violinists, who never failed to come over to our table, played to us as only a gypsy with his violin can.

Before the Gates of Armageddon

If it had not been for the chain of events that brought on the first World War, the summer of 1914 would have been a time of thanksgiving throughout Europe and the Balkans, for nature smiled on the land that year. The cattle were fat and sleek, the wheat ripened to a golden bounty, and the yields from orchard and vineyard gave cause for rejoicing. We were on tour in the Balkans and had come to Zagreb, the historic capital city of the then Austro-Hungarian province of Croatia-Slavonia, for a long summer stand, and were there on the 28th of June. That was the date on which an assassin's bullets ignited the fuse to a powderkeg, which was an armed and divided Europe. It happened in

---

* The cymbalom, a descendant of the ancient dulcimer and psaltery, is a four-octave metal string instrument used in gypsy orchestras.

the city of Sarajevo, in the province of Bosnia, not more than 200 miles southeast of Zagreb as the crow flies. The assassin was a Servian (Serbian) and the victims were the heir-apparent to the throne of the Hapsburgs, the Archduke Franz Ferdinand, and his consort, the Duchess Sophie of Hohenberg. They were on a state visit.

In Zagreb, business went on as usual, although there was an undercurrent of anxiety during those fateful July days, as the people watched for the latests bulletins and learned of the deepening crisis. The cable cars were going back and forth between the upper and lower towns, and the scenes in Maximer Park and the Botanical Gardens were those of people finding relief from the heat in the dog days of a Balkan summer. There was talk of war, of course, but a reluctance to envisage it, so the people of Zagreb gave rein to their hopes and sought escape from their fears in the diverting atmosphere of the circus. The reverberations from those shots at Sarajevo could not be stifled, however. The nations bristled before the gates of Armageddon, and when Austria-Hungary declared war on the Kingdom of Servia (later Serbia) on July 28, the gates opened wide and drew the world in. An order for general mobilization came quickly. Reservists began rushing to the colors, the railroads were taken over by the army, and transportation, other than for the conveyance of troops, came to a stop in all the Hapsburg lands.

Back to Budapest—The Hard Way

We had come to Zagreb from Budapest by rail with splended new caravans; our horses and ponies, elephants, camels, zebras, and bears; our tents and heavy equipment, and a considerable personnel. Now we would have to go back by road: not by the well-traveled main roads, from which we were barred by the military, but by little used, indirect, and narrow back-roads, which were often nothing but wagon trails. We would have to wend our way northeastward through a wild region of ravines and mountain grades along the forested slopes of the Warasdin and Kalnik mountains in Croatia-Slavonia and beyond the Drave to the Hungarian plain, where it would be hot and dry in the deep of summer and the dust would blow. We could cool off, perhaps, on the shores of Lake Balaton. It would be a long way.

At a time when our immediate departure was imperative to avoid internment, army agents came to the circus and commandeered a number of our draft horses, thus seriously reducing our means of transportation. About half of our caravans and a good part of our heavy equipment would have to be left behind, in the hope of getting it back after the war, which most people thought would be a short one. We would have to depart at once with the wagons and caravans for which we had horses, leading and driving our animals on the long trek back to Budapest. There would be a lot of walking. At the last minute, the military authorities made a railroad car available to the women, and before dawn of the next day we left Zagreb on the banks of the Save, homeward bound.

No strangers to difficult undertakings, and being young, we made adventure, if not actually a lark, out of the strenuous two weeks it took to make the journey. The way was rough, narrow, and meandering. In the mountains it ascended circuitously at steep grades, now descending to follow the course of a swift moving stream in the bed of a deep gorge, only to point skyward again in another long, winding ascent. Before reaching the Hungarian plain, where it was hot and dry and the dust blew in clouds, we passed through a valley where the rain came down in torrents. The heavily loaded wagons sank into the mud and became mired down beyond the power of the horses to extricate. Two of our elephants, mature cows, were veterans in harness and experienced in taking over from the horses in a bog-down. So we put them to work. Crouching low to get under the load, they applied their strength, and with seeming ease pulled the wagons out of the gumbo in the creek bed to higher ground, while the horses rested.

Before leaving Zagreb, we gave the feet of our elephants a thorough manicure, taking care to leave enough of the pad for the protection of the inner foot against the hard, rough, and possibly stony surfaces in prospect. And we trimmed and shaped the nails—for the same reason. Elephants in the circus do no great amount of walking, as a rule, so the pads on their feet have to be trimmed down periodically and kept straight. If we had not always followed this practice, we would have had some sore-footed elephants and even some crippled ones to deal with before reaching our goal.

In one of the wagons we carried a liberal supply of bran and raw linseed oil, to feed to the elephants in the form of a mash, in the event of digestive troubles, to which they are subject. In another wagon we had a sealed barrel of cognac, or something closely akin to it. This was not necessarily for the elephants, but it would have been given to them had they developed chills from a sudden drop of temperature, such as could be expected in the mountains. Elephants develop a great passion for intoxicants, so it is a good thing they are not in a position to help themselves.

The unheralded appearance of our strange cavalcade created a stir in the more remote villages, in which few of the inhabitants had ever gazed upon such a sight. Sustained only by their curiosity, some of them stood by in wary astonishment. Others ran to cover, the Chinese and the dark-skinned North Africans we had with us proving too frightening to their unaccustomed eyes. The consternation in a few places was such that the police saw fit to escort us through. During the heat of the noon-day we stopped to rest the horses, and in the evenings, when we came to a place where we could find barns or a courtyard in which to quarter the animals, were only too glad to settle down for the night. On our wagons, we carried big, raft-like wooden platforms for the elephants, at both ends of which there were heavy iron rings. Removing the platforms from the wagons, we would put them down at some selected place, preferably a meadow, stake them in, and secure the pachyderms, one to each platform, by chaining them from one front leg and the opposite hind leg to the rings.

Back in Budapest at last, as the first battles of the war were raging, we brought our foot-weary column to a halt at the Cirkus Barogaldi and there quartered our animals. Budapest was the scene now of marching soldiery and of crowds milling with martial enthusiasm along the avenues and boulevards in flag-waving but tearful farewell to the departing troops. Young soldiers they were, the very flower of Hungary's youth. Many of them never came back. Within a few days, an epidemic of cholera broke out in Kaschau, a hundred miles or so to the northeast. The authorities commandeered our tents and ordered us to go to the stricken city to put the tents up for the hospitalization of the sick. People were dying like flies in Kaschau, but modern methods of sanitation and immunization brought the plague under control.

During the summer of 1914 I became a correspondent, which was unusual for me. My letters were to Manya, of course, and she wrote to me. On returning to Budapest from Zagreb with our circus, we began working with a number of our acts in the Barogaldi. The Guttenberg Reiterei were still there, so my romance with Manya was renewed under the eloquent circumstance of our two families working together in the same circus.

Manya and I resumed our trysts in the Varosliget and on Oct. 1, 1914, we were married. Thereafter, within a few days Adolph was inducted into the cavalry, and Max and I were inducted and assigned to the infantry, with orders to go at once to Trentschin for training. Sandor was beyond the age limit for active service, but he entered the army as a volunteer and served in a non-combative capacity. Oscar was under age in 1914, but was taken by the army in 1917 and saw active service in the last year of the war. With the exception of Alfons, who went to Santiago, Chile, in 1913 with an acrobatic troupe and became a citizen, all of us served in the Austro-Hungarian army. By an unusual happenstance, Max and I and, later on, Oscar, were members of the same regiment, the 71st, and were in active

service on the Serbian and Roumanian fronts. Adolph was on
the Italian front.

Ten days before the end of the war—the catastrophic end of
it, for Austria-Hungary—I was granted a furlough to go home
for a few days. On entering the concourse of the railroad station in Budapest, where we detrained, I found myself in the
midst of a vast crowd of noisy, shouting soldiery, and before I
knew what had happened the insignia were ripped from my
tunic, as a gray-coated private said to me:

"You don't need these any more. The war is over." I thought
I was in a revolution, but I soon learned that the war really was
over. Returning to my unit, when my furlough was up, I was
ordered to Trentschin, this time to be mustered out.

The four long, grinding years of war terminated an era,
changed everything, or almost everything, and brought about
the dismemberment of Austria-Hungary. Max lost his life in the
war. My father died in 1916, so was spared much. With the de-
mobilization of the Austro-Hungarian armies, Adolph, Oscar,
and I returned to Budapest, a changed and despairing city.

All our animals, with the exception of a few half-starved
horses and ponies, were gone. Food had been scarce and there
was none for them. Yet a circus and circuses there had to be.
Though their ranks had been thinned, there were still plenty of
artistes. Troupes that had disappeared in the war days had re-
organized and were seeking employment. Others would be seen
no more. There was more need now than ever for the kind of di-
version and entertainment the circus affords, so, after having
obtained a lease of the Municipal Circus at the zoo in the Varosliget, we began the business of putting a circus together again.
It was 1919.

Under the Red Heel: The Scourge of Bela Kun

Hungary's was a bitter cup in the years after the World War.
The casualties and privations of the struggle had brought this
excellent but ill-fated little country to a low ebb. The loss of

vital territories, further impoverishment and demoralization, the wages of defeat in war did the rest, and provided the Communists with a fertile field in which to begin their work. There were Communists among the returning prisoners of war from Russia, and at their head was the Transylvania-born fanatic Bela Kun, fresh from a course of training in the tactics of Communist revolution in Moscow.

The postwar People's Republic under Count Mihaly Karolyi temporized. It was weak in decision and slow to understand, and in March, 1919, woke up to find itself the captive of a Red hard core under the lash of Bela Kun. The Communists were comparatively few in numbers but expert in the exploitation of unrest, which was widespread and deep-seated. When once in the seat of power, they revealed their purpose, which was to impose on Hungary an exact pattern of 1917 Soviet Communism.

"Lenin's ruffians," as they were called, who arrested, tortured and executed people on their own authority, were turned loose on the city. The old courts of law were done away with and revolutionary tribunals were set up in their place. All private property was declared to be the property of the state, Communists were quartered on middle class families, 400 distinguished citizens were taken as hostages, and a policy of terror was proclaimed as an instrument of government.

That the Communists had seized power was made known to us one evening in the early spring of 1919 when a cohort of revolutionists, accompanied by armed guards, came to the Municipal Circus after the performance and demanded to see us. Upon our coming into their presence, the orator of the group denounced us as bourgeoisie and "enemies of the people." We were under arrest, he declared, and would be tried that night in the People's Court. If convicted, we would be shot in the morning. The count against us was simply that we were members of the property-owning middle class, and we were given to understand that everything we owned was to be confiscated.

The tirade of abuse and condemnation went on in this vein

into the gray hours of the morning, at which time our visitors
departed, leaving us alone, but under guard, until the dawn
ripened into day. Then they returned. Our trial had been delayed, they said, and our prosecution would be withheld, if we
would agree to stay on in the circus in cooperation with the
"new management." Thereupon, a group of sinister looking men
filed in and were introduced to us as the "new managers" of the
People's Circus, by authority of the people's commissars of the
Hungarian Soviet government. They were renegades of one
kind or another, and several had the kind of physiognomy one
might expect to see in the penitentiary or in the shadows of the
underworld. Among them were some of our stable hands, including one we had fired for good cause.

A few weeks later, word reached us that the man we employed as manager, whose name was Wildman, had been killed.
He and his wife lived comfortably in a five-room apartment near
the Varosliget. After removing him as the manager and replac-
ing him with a Communist henchman, the revolutionaries quartered some of their own people on him in his apartment, taking
four of the rooms and forcing Wildman and his wife to live in
the one room. Wildman's wife lived to tell how he died.

On returning to their apartment one evening, the Wildmans
found the place locked against them. Presently the door opened
from the inside.

"Where do you think you're going?", challenged one of the
Communists. Wildman replied that he and his wife would like
to go to their room.

"Oh, would you?" said the Communist, as he stood across
the Wildmans' path. Wildman remonstrated. The Communist
drew a revolver and fired, and Wildman fell dead.

Rags and Bloody Feet

For a period of 132 days, which was the duration of the dic-
tatorship, we worked like animals under the goad of the "new
government," performing every afternoon and evening before

Communist-packed audiences, with the guards of the despotism standing by. Deprived of our homes and possessions in Budapest, and assigned to wretched one-room flats, we were paid in fiat money, called "white" money, which was worthless. Having no clothes other than what we had on our backs, we were soon in rags, so we appealed to the "managers," who denounced us for doing so and laughed hilariously at our appearance. One day it was announced that a truck with a load of miscellaneous clothing had arrived at the circus. On going out to the truck, however, we were held back and admonished of the fact that in "the People's State" the workers had first choice. They did have.

The grooms, keepers, and other menial employees, many of whom had been brought in by the Communists, swarmed all over the truck, and when they got through helping themselves there was nothing left.

Our need for clothes finally became so desperate that an assortment of suits, coats, and other garments was allotted. All of it was made of an *ersatz* material, however, which was not much better than paper. In the meantime, our shoes were so far gone that we were walking on bloody feet. New shoes were given us at length, but we were not much better off, because they had wooden soles and didn't fit anyway.

One day it rained. The flat my wife and baby son and I occupied was five miles from the circus, so I had to walk that distance in the rain. By the time I arrived at my destination, my *ersatz* suit had shrunken tight, and was coming apart at the seams. I was arrested, tried before a revolutionary tribunal on a charge of indecent exposure, and fined a week's pay.

The revolutionary tribunals were in continuous session all over the city, and the one that had been set up at the circus held sessions every night after the show. To that tribunal we were summoned time and again on concocted charges. It was dangerous to be late, whatever the reason, or to be ill, as my wife learned. For having been too ill to work on one occasion, she was arrested, fined, and subjected to the usual indignities.

Who are your friends? To our eternal gratitude, that question was answered in the time of Bela Kun by the deeds of those who saved our lives. One of our friends was a captain of the police. He gave me an old suit. It was too big for me, but it was warm. Another was a butcher. He gave us meat. And there was the old gardener and handy man. Now and then he slipped us a bottle of milk and brought us provisions in the darkness of the night, a sack of potatoes and a bag of flour. There were others. Some of them we didn't even know. They were just people who loved the circus and who remembered us and knew our need.

As the members of a successful, circus-owning family, as members of the property-owning middle class, therefore, we were marked for destruction and lost everything. The trunks in which we kept the treasured photographs, records, and varied and sundry mementos of our heritage as an old circus family, the medals, awards, and gifts that had been presented to my parents and to the rest of us, all these were taken from our apartments and we never saw them again.

In 1912, at Stryj, in Galicia, on the first of July, we put on a special performance for the Archduke Karl Franz Joseph and the Archduchess Zita and entourage. It was a command performance, and, in token of his appreciation, the Archduke, then a young man of 25, presented diamond and ruby-studded watches, chains, and stick pins to each one of my brothers and to me. The Communists took these, of course.

With counter-revolution threatening in the provinces, where massacres of the peasants had occurred, the Bela Kun Communists fled Budapest before Roumanian armies, which came in, rough-shod, and occupied the country. Roumanian troops were quartered on the cities, which they plundered, carrying off machinery, railroad rolling stock, busses, scientific material and equipment from the hospitals and universities, and even the furnishings of the hotels and former private dwellings. On the heels of the Roumanians, who withdrew under Allied pressure, Senegalese Africans under French command came in. The very black Senegalese were feared and resented. There were instances, and plenty of rumors, of assault and rapine, but the French officers maintained discipline and there was nothing like the plundering of the Roumanians.

The winter months of the following year, 1920, which were cold and hard, found us destitute and half-starved. I shoveled snow for a living and hauled firewood and coal, with a sad old horse hitched to a wagon, from dawn to dusk for weeks on end. With the departure of the Senegalese divisions and the re-establishment of something resembling order by counter-revolutionary veterans under the command of Admiral Horthy, we managed to get up out of out inertia and once again to begin reorganizing a circus. Performers and others who had worked for us began coming back, the Communist grooms and keepers among them, looking for work, and before long we were able to begin providing the relief in entertainment for which there was an acute need.

V

A Life Raft to the Drowning

We Go to Italy

IT WAS 1920, and in the once gay and lustrous city of Budapest there was little more than despair and destitution. A light appeared in the gloom, however, when a man from Rome came to see us. As agent for the partners B & D of that city, he had just negotiated the purchase of what remained of the circus of Matthias Beketow, and wanted to retain our services as equestrians and directors. We were to take charge of the liberty horses and ponies, tents, and caravans that had been purchased from Beketow, to procure the talent and all additional equipment necessary for a complete circus, and to take the same, together with our own horses, to Italy.

This was like the appearance of a life raft before the eyes of the drowning. We accepted the offer, and, in due course, which was none too soon, Adolph and his wife Lilly, Manya and I and our small son Alexander, with a circus in our charge, boarded the train that was to take us into the sunlight of a new life. Sandor chose to remain in Budapest.

We detrained at Udine, the native city of Antoine Franconi, who went to France in 1758 and became the founder of the celebrated Franconi family of equestrians and circus directors.

Stones, Riots and Strikes In Italy

The Socialists were in power in Italy in 1920. Some hundreds of factories had been seized by the workers, only to be handed back to the owners in disillusionment, and the revolutionary spirit was finding release in street demonstrations. Mussolini had already organized the first of the Fascio di Combattimento, but the "March on Rome" and the establishment of a Fascist government were a year and a half away.

From Udine we set forth on a tour of Lombardy, Venetia, Emilia, and Tuscany, and ran into trouble on the narrow streets of Brescia, where we were literally driven out of town before a shower of stones and such imprecations as "Nemici! Nemici!" ("Enemy! Enemy!") and "Ungherese andate a casa!" (Hungarians, go home!").

This was supposed to have been a spontaneous manifestation of hostility toward us, the directors, because we were Hungarians, allies of the Austrians and enemies, therefore, of Italy. However, we were later given grounds for suspecting that the incident had been inspired by agitators from within the circus who were conspiring to take our jobs. There were a few subsequent demonstrations of this nature along the route, but none of them had the violence of the Brescian incident.

In addition to acting as directors of the circus, we trained and presented the liberty horses, Adolph rode the high-school, and we worked together—Adolph, Lilly, Manya, and I—in our bareback act. In Florence, Rome, Milan, and Bologna we showed in permanent circus buildings, but in Treviso, Pistoia, Pisa, and Venice we were a tenting show.

As we began a two-week engagement in the Teatro Florentino, in Florence, a civil war seemed about to break out. Florence, like other cities of Italy's industrial north, was a center of Communist strength and had been plagued with Communist-inspired strikes and other disturbances. It was in the spring of 1921, the year in which Fascism began making its bid for power, and street fighting between the Communists and Mussolini's Fascisti was occurring. We began our performance on schedule, but on the fourth day the lights went out, so the circus had to shut down. Against a background of sporadic rifle fire and other tell-tale explosions, all normal activity within the city came to a stop. Four or five days passed before municipal services were restored and the circus could resume its engagement. At this time the Fascist fighters put into effect their technique of branding Communists on their foreheads and administering large doses of castor oil.

They Came in Gondolas

In Venice the circus was conducted on the green-meadowed islet of Santa Elena, and the people came to it in gondolas and other boats. High winds swept the islet on our arrival there and continued blowing for several days. The "big top" collapsed two times in a row and everything had to be fastened down by tie and stake. After the second blow-down, we decided to play in the open. The winds favored us by dying away, and for the rest of our week-long engagement we held circus under blue Venetian skies in the afternoons and the star-studded heavens at night. The views across the blue waters surrounding us were unforgettable, especially in the golden light at sundown and during the twilight that lingered. At that time, Venice was transformed into a jeweled city of the story books. The waters from which it seemed to rise took on the hues of a magic world as the gold gave way to amethyst and rose.

The supply of hay we were able to ferry to the circus was limited and it was soon gone. But that did not matter because the grass was plentiful and succulent on the islet of Santa Elena. Oats were difficult of procurement in that watery, warm-shadowed region of islets, lagoons, canals, bridges, gondolas, and painted sails. We bought a quantity of dried bread instead, and hat it conveyed to the circus by water.

How many people know that horses will take to dried bread with a relish and grow fat on it?

How My Nose Acquired Its Present Shape

Toward the end of our Italian tour in B & D's Circo Beketow, Oscar joined us to do his trick roping and broncho-busting in an American Wild West Show act we improvised for Italian consumption. The climax of this feature was a gun battle between cowboys and Indians, in which my horse and I went through the routine of being shot. One of our "Indians" fired two blanks at the horse and one at me, whereupon the horse went down and I rolled off the saddle. I was "wounded," of course, and, staggering to my feet, brought a hand to my forehead, at the same time opening up a vial of blood-red paint, which streaked down my face and saturated my shirt front.

One night my "Indian" assailant got mixed up and fired a third blank at the horse, while the horse was in process of going down, as he was supposed to, and before I had rolled clear from the saddle. This was when my nose got its present shape. The third blank, which was fired at close range, frightened the horse. The horse bolted, and, lunging upward, struck me hard in the face with his head, shattering my nose and laying it open. The gore was real this time, and the Red Cross men had an actual casualty to give aid to, as they came into the ring in their wagon to pick up the casualties of the mock battle. My whole face turned a deep red and black and blue from the smash, and became a painful, pulsating torment to me for days.

That reminds me of Frank Eders and his wife Elza, who were friends of ours in the circus. Frank was an Austrian weight juggler who bounced iron balls off his chest. Elza was of an old family of circus *artistes*, and I had known her since childhood. Elza had always been strong, and as youngsters she and I used to engage in rough but good-natured play. She and her daughter, who was just a young girl, had a trapeze act in the Circo Beketow; the daughter was the trapezist and performed on a triangle, which her mother held. Since we knew the Eders so well, we saw a great deal of them on the Italian tour, in the course of which Elza and I still engaged in the horse-play we had indulged in at a more becoming age. The black eye amused her. "Now, now, now, look what we have here," exclaimed Elza when she beheld it, along with the patched up, splinted nose, and the painfully discolored face I had got in the Wild West show.

"And you say the horse hit you, Arthur? Who do you think you can fool with that explanation? Don't be silly, Arthur, isn't it about time you learned not to fight with a man who is bigger than you are?"

With that we both forgot our ages.

"Careful, shrimp!" said Elza. "I'm bigger and stronger than I used to be."

Reacting just as I had to her tomboy challenges of former years, I said:

"Elza, do you remember how I once picked you up and put you on your back?"

"Oh, so," she replied, "and that didn't happen often, did it?"

The challenge was too much. We tangled, and in the tussle that followed, the matronly but strong and still agile Elza slipped, collided with a table corner, and came up with the makings of a full, round black eye.

That night, when the Eders, Manya, and I went out together for a little relaxation after the performance, Frank said to his wife: "If you think I am going to be seen walking alongside a woman with a 'shiner' like that, you are mistaken. It will be rumored around that I have taken to beating you. I can't afford to let that happen."

Manya took up the banter by saying: "How right you are.

And I don't want it said that I struck my husband with a crow-
bar. Come, Frank, to protect our reputations, you and I will
walk together."

A few moments later Frank turned around, and, looking dis-
dainfully at Elza and me, said to Manya:

"Manya, dear, what a fine home life that pair must lead."

"Poor Arthur," exclaimed Elza.

"Poor Elza," said I, as we beheld each other.

And, with that, we all began to laugh, uncontrollably, until I
could feel the throb of every pulse beat in my poor aching face.

Conspiracy in the Circus

The stoning in Brescia and other pointed but less compelling
demonstrations along the way had seemed to imply the existence of an organized hostility toward us within the circus. But
we were not alert to an active conspiracy until a few weeks before we arrived in Rome.

At that time, one of the *artistes,* a woman, who was a strong
friend of ours, informed us of what was afoot. She had been approached by one of the conspirators, who sought to enlist her
collaboration. Her first thought, she said, was to denounce the
scheme and all who were parties to it, but, on second thought
she decided to feign approval, so that she might keep abreast
of the situation and be in a position to keep us informed.

Certain performers and a few disgruntled employees had
entered into a conspiracy with the partners of B & D to break
the contract and to get rid of us. They were moved by professional jealousy and had been chiding the quite susceptible
B & D about the amount of money they were paying us under
the contract. Get rid of the Konyots, they suggested, and we
will conduct the show for you just as well as the Konyots and
for less money. The partners were unhappy as well, we learned,
with the clause in the contract under which they were obligated
to pay us a month in advance. So the conspiracy not to observe
that clause, and by not doing so to precipitate a misunderstand-

ing, was enjoined. It had been the custom to pay us on the regularly recurring due dates immediately after the evening
performance, and the plan was to withhold the money on the
next one.

The conspirators had laid their plans carefully, but they had
overlooked an important fact. The part of Hungary to which
we were native had been ceded to the newly constituted state
of Czecho-Slovakia, which gave us the status of Czecho-Slovak
nationals, instead of Hungarians. As such, therefore, we went to
the Czecho-Slovak consul-general in Rome and told him all
about the conspiracy that was being hatched.

"Keep mum," he said, "and avoid any indication that you are
aware of anything. Go to the circus, as usual, on the appointed
evening, but do not dress for the performance."

He, the consul-general would wait until about half an hour
before the opening and would then go to B & D and tell them
that he had learned about the scheme and that he was acting
to protect our interest, as, indeed, he was bound to, for the reason that we were Czecho-Slovak nationals. He had instructed
us, he would tell them, not to perform in our usual capacities
until they, B & D, had deposited with him the money that was
due us under the terms of the contract.

When thus apprised, B & D professed innocence. But our
reasons for believing that they not only knew about it but were
a party to it were convincing. In the meantime, the amphitheatre had become full, and when the show did not begin on time,
the audience grew restive. Shouting demands were raised that
their money be returned, and disorder threatened. The show
did not begin, of course, since we were the directors of it, and
would not proceed until we had been given our month's pay in
advance, and this time before the show and not after it. The
compulsion on B & D was, in these circumstances, irresistible,
with the result that they gave way, and, in compliance with his
insistence, gave the counsul-general the pay we had coming to
us.

With that accomplished, we took up our duties, and, in accordance with the consul-general's instructions, made our acts as usual that night. But that was the end, for as soon as B & D's treacherous intentions became known to us, we had procured a booking in Paris with the Nouveau Cirque, which was to take effect at an early date.

So it was now on to Paris, with our horses, our personal effects, and our money. We would have to get across the border first, however.

One of the horses we had with us when we arrived at the French border was a young one I had bought in Tuscany for high-school training. The Italian customs officers, having been falsely informed by B & D that I was not the legal owner of this horse, challenged me to prove ownership and refused to give clearance until I had done so. B & D were proceeding on the theory, apparently, that I might not have troubled to provide myself with a bill of sale covering the purchase of this horse, in which they were mistaken. However, in the excitement of our last days in Rome I had neglected to include this bill of sale with the papers and documents we would need for presentation at the border. Nor could I remember where or in which one of our many trunks and packing boxes I had packed it. B & D knew of our Nouveau Cirque engagement and hoped to delay us long enough at the border to preclude our arriving in Paris at the contractually prescribed date, which would place us in default.

They didn't succeed, but they did cause us a distressing amount of trouble and some anxious moments. Fortunately, while in the midst of unpacking and rummaging through our trunks in search of the missing paper, I happened to remember the name of the man from whom I bought the horse, and the town in Tuscany where he lived. I was able to reach him by telephone and to get from him the required release, which he sent by telegram. The Italian customs officers were, therewith, obliged to let us across the border to proceed on our journey to Paris.

VI

France and North Africa

Five Years in the French Circus

ON CONCLUDING our engagement in the Nouveau Cirque in Paris, we went to Germany on a three month contract with Hans Stosch-Sarassani in Dresden and Frankfort, and, returning to France, spent nearly five years in the French circus.

Through four consecutive seasons, from spring to fall, we were on the road all over France in the Cirque Napoleon Rancy. Two winters were consumed on tour in North Africa, in the Cirque Albert Rancy and the Cirque Caroli, respectively, and two in Paris in the Cirque Medrano. Prior to going to Spain in the fall of 1926, we were in the Cirque d'Hiver in Paris.

No city in the world has a richer tradition of the circus than Paris. In the 1850's, Paris was the Mecca and hub of the continental circus world. From the 1840's through the 1880's, moreover, it was the very center of classical horsemanship. Foremost among the personages who were responsible for this ascendency were the Italian-born Antoine Franconi (1738-1836), and his descendents, and the renowned Francois Baucher (1796-1873),

55

a former trick rider, who won fame as a master of the *haute école*. Baucher created the cult of the *écuyére* in Paris, i.e., the beauteous, top-hatted young horsewoman with the hour-glass figure and the flowing black skirt, who rode *en haute école* in the side-saddle and performed feats of daring in such historic circuses as the Olympique, the Moliere, the d'Ete, and the d'Hiver. The latter was originally the Napoleon.

The first of Baucher's pupils in this most glamorous of epochs in the Parisian circus was the dark-eyed Caroline Loyo. Loyo made her debut in 1833 in the Cirque Olympique, went to England, where, it is recorded, she brought London to her feet, and became the darling thereafter of the fashionable world in France. She was followed closely by the lame but lovely Pauline Cuzent, whose grace and reputedly bewitching charms were said to have been "infinite." Emilie Loisett, of a famous equestrian family and a niece of Caroline Loyo, came afterward. Loisett, known in her time as "the Patti" of the *haute école,* was fatally injured in an accident in the Cirque d'Hiver while still in her 20's.

Incident in the Cirque Medrano

Of the many arenas that contributed to the luster of the circus in Paris, only the Cirque d'Hiver and the Medrano remain. The Medrano got its name from a Spaniard, who began his circus career as an acrobatic clown, and, like Matthias Beketow of Budapest, did his clowning with a trained pig in tow. On his first appearance in France, so the story goes, Medrano was working in the Cirque Fernando, and in coming on to the stage announced himself with a resounding "Boum! Boum!" From that time on, for the rest of his life, he was known as "Boum Boum." Medrano died before his time, and the directorship of his circus passed into the capable hands of M. Bonton, who, upon the death of Mme. Medrano, became the guardian of the Medranos' young son, Jerome.

It was during the time of M. Bonton, in the winter of 1923,

that we suffered our last encounter with the hostile feeling still harbored by the French as a result of the 1914-1918 war. On this occasion, upon our coming into the ring with our bareback horses, there were cries of "Boches!" M. Bonton rose to the occasion and spoke aloud to the demonstrators.

"These people are Hungarians," he protested, "and not Boches."

"Pfui!" came the retort. "Allies of the Boches, that's what they were."

It looked as though we were in for a rough evening as the demonstration continued. Cries of "Enemies of France, go home!" and "Tell the Hungarians to go to Germany!" were hurled from every direction in what seemed a mounting chorus. But Bonton stood his ground and from his box shouted back reprovingly:

"Shame on you! You disgrace your country. Gentlemen do not insult people who are here as *artistes* and guests of this nation. If you are Frenchmen, you will stop this disgraceful exhibition at once."

The uproar subsided and an eloquent stillness came over the arena. M. Bonton had met the demonstrators head-on and shamed them into silence.

In the fall of 1922, M. Bonton sent me on a 14-day furlough to Hungary and Germany to bring back two horses from Budapest, Reingold and Mausie, which I still owned, and to procure harnesses and other equipment for his liberty horses.

Association with the Rancys

Our association with the Rancy family, equestrians and circus proprietors, was long and pleasant. The Rancys came into prominence so long ago that it doesn't matter when. Theodore was apparently the first of them, and the date of his birth is given as 1818. Of him it is recorded that he rode *en haute école* in 1850 at the Cirque des Champs Elysées, in Paris, and that he did so without bridle or saddle.

From the beginning, the Rancys have been travelers. Rouen was their home city, and it was from there that the Cirque Napoleon Rancy went out on its annual travels. The first European circus to tour Egypt was owned and directed by a Rancy. That was in 1868 during the inauguration of the Suez Canal.

In France, Adolph formed his own bareback troupe, which included Lilly, of course. Meanwhile, Manya's brothers, John and Rudolph, and her sisters, Adele and Stella, joined us to form a troupe of six. Our work in the Cirque Napoleon Rancy was not confined to bareback riding, however. Manya and I both rode the high-school, and a good deal of my own time was spent training high-school and liberty horses. I taught Napoleon Rancy's son Henri to ride the high-school and his daughter Dora to make a sulky act, in which the horse, driven in a high two-wheeled cart, performed the movements of the high-school in harness. After a year or so, Henri and I made a double high-school act. The liberty horses I trained included a sextette of grays and a sextette of chestnuts, which we later combined to make an outstanding liberty act of 12. Several years later, at the Olympia in London, the Rancys made an act said to have been originated by the great Ducrow,* in which eight horses are controlled by a lone rider, seven of them from the back of one. In Hungary this is called a *czikospost*.

It was during this five-year period that we made two expeditions to North Africa, the first one with the Cirque Albert Rancy and the second with the Cirque Caroli. The itineraries, involving a total of 14 months, were wide-ranging, and included Rabat, Casablanca, and Marrakesh, in Morocco; Oran, Sidi-Bel-Abbes, and Setif, in Algeria, and Tunis, Gabes, Bizerte, Susa, and Sfax, in Tunisia.

On one occasion, on a starry night at an oasis in the Sahara desert, we put on a show for a sheik in the courtyard of his harem, which was in the middle of a palm grove.

* Andrew Ducrow (1793-1842), equestrian acrobat of fabulous accomplishments. Succeeded to management of Philip Astley's Hippodrome in London on the death of Astley's son John in 1821. Developed the equestrian spectacles initiated by Astley and created new ones. Son of a French vaulter and strong man.

No, we did not see the sheik's women, whose view of the circus was obtained through narrow apertures in the walls of their seclusion.

Oscar Konyot, Rider, Trainer and Circus Director

During the tour of North Africa with the Cirque Albert Rancy, Oscar and I were together again for some four or five months, after having been out of touch for several years. From the beginning, like the rest of our family, Oscar was a bareback rider, in which connection it will be recalled that as a young boy in 1909, 1910, and 1911, while we were in the United States with Barnum & Bailey, he became a member of our bareback troupe in the disguise of a girl. Over the years he also became an expert all-around horseman and a skilled animal trainer, as well. More to the point, in his cowboy riding and all that goes with it, he developed a forte that was uniquely his own. It was to organize and conduct a Wild West show, as a feature of the Cirque Albert Rancy, that he came to North Africa. Beyond that, and quite aside from it, the trials, whereabouts and achievements of Oscar Konyot in the 1920's make an interesting story, so I shall recount them.

Oscar left Budapest in 1920, soon after we did, and went to Italy, broke and hungry. He was a highly capable trick rider, of course, but he had no horse.

In Italy, he worked in a few small circuses, using one of the circus horses for his lassoeing, rope-spinning, and whip-cracking, which he did with a pair of bull whips. This led to a contract with the Circo Almart in 1923 as equestrian director, in which capacity he took charge of 40 liberty, trick, and high-school horses. The North African engagement followed. In France, thereafter, working in various French circuses over a period of seven years with his cowboy act, he became widely known as a rider of bucking horses, American style, excepting for the fact that he mounted the bucking horse on stage without a shute. Cowboys, how about that?

Of the numerous horses Oscar used in his trick-riding and cowboy work, he likes best to tell about Lola, an Arabian mare he trained to race a motor bike. This little mare was remarkably fast and handy and could best a motor bike in an arena or enclosure only 13 yards wide. She could break into a full gallop immediately from a dead stand and come to a stop again almost instantly after 13 yards. On an open road she could give the motor bike a 50-yard start and still pass it. Lola was a feature attraction and a favorite performer with audiences at various sport shows throughout France.

For the Circo Arbel in Bologna, Italy, Oscar trained horses for the owner and presented his cowboy act. He also gave the owner's children instructions in bareback and trick riding. In the meantime, the two Dell 'Acqua brothers, circus performers and friends of Oscar's in southern Italy, came into possession of a circus. They were in good financial standing, but the circus was a poor affair, and the brothers were short on knowledge of the circus world, so they called Oscar in.

"Here, Oscar," they said, "you have a circus. We are only performers. You do what you want."

The Circo Dell 'Acqua, if it could be called a circus, had little more in the way of equipment than a "big top" full of holes. It had three horses, one of which was so old that he couldn't keep his tongue in his mouth. The second was a liberty horse, and the third was an unbroken four-year-old stallion. Oscar sent the old horse to the market, where he brought 500 lira, which had an exchange value of 85 cents. He took the stallion into the act the next day.

A few new animals and a new "big top" were then bought, and from this beginning a circus was developed in which there were liberty and high-school acts, a liberty act with camels, and acts with bears and lions. In six years the Circo Dell 'Acqua became the biggest circus in Italy, but more important even than this achievement was the fact that Oscar's experience with the lions in the Circo Dell 'Acqua started him off on his career as a lion trainer, in which capacity he was to become celebrated.

Lottie and Prinz

In 1922, in Dresden, Germany, while in the Zirkus Sarassani,
I bought a pair of miniature German pinschers, Lottie and Prinz.
Bright little things, weighing only one and one-half and just over
two pounds, respectively, they were silky, short-coated black
and tans. Lottie became Manya's and Prinz was mine. They
were brim full of character and jealously affectionate, both of
them, and we took them with us wherever we went.

Every year the Cirque Napoleon Rancy stopped at the port
city of Marseilles for a three-week stand, and when we came
there in that circus in 1922 Lottie and Prinz were with us, of
course. On the road in France, we stayed in hotels and our little
pinschers went to the circus with us every day. Lottie's post was
on the trunk in Manya's dressing room and Prinz settled down
on the trunk in mine. During the performances they remained
there in the dressing rooms, well triggered little alarums, on
guard and poised to fly at any and all intruders.

On the last night of the Marseilles engagement in 1922, when
I returned to my dressing room after our act, Prinz was not
there. I called him, and searched the area, calling, but there was
no response and no sign of Prinz. I notified the *gendarmerie*,
who publicized the disappearance. I put an advertisement in
the newspapers and offered a reward, leaving the money with
the policemen to be paid to the finder. We had to be on our way
that night in the circus. The months rolled by, and not a word
did I have. My Prinz was gone, probably forever, and I resigned
myself to that unhappy fact.

A year later the Cirque Napoleon Rancy returned to Marseilles. On the day of our arrival, after having taken our luggage
to the hotel and unpacked it, we hired a cab to drive us to the
circus grounds. Within a block or so from the circus a big man
appeared on the sidewalk with a tiny little black and tan dog
following him, just as Prinz used to follow me. In obedience to
my direction, the cab driver drove up closer to the big man and

the little dog that looked so like Prinz. At a distance of about 100 yards I got out and began calling, "Prinzie! Prinzie! Prinzie!" With alacrity, the little black and tan turned in his tracks, came running toward me, and jumped with whimpering delight into my arms. I had found my Prinzie.

The man from whom I had taken my dog was all of six feet, four inches in height. He was proportionately broad and not less strong because of his trade, which was that of a brick mason.

"Hey, you," he shouted at me in a booming voice, "stop calling my dog."

"He is not your dog," I replied. "He is my dog. Someone stole him from my dressing room in this circus in Marseilles a year ago."

A *gendarme* at the near corner, on hearing the altercation, came over to investigate. I told him my story, and he said he was on duty in this same vicinity the year before and remembered the disappearance of the dog from the circus.

"Where did you get the dog," he asked the man, and the man said, "I found him."

"Well, then, when you found him," asked the *gendarme*, "why didn't you report your finding him?"

Thereupon, the man turned to me and said, "All right, so I found him. But I didn't know whose dog he was. I have been feeding him for a year now, so you owe me for the feed."

"That's a good one," I said. "You steal my dog and keep him for a year and then have the audacity to tell me I owe you money for feeding him."

The *gendarme* had had enough, so he ordered the man to be on his way, if he didn't want to be arrested and thrown into jail.

After the last performance of the Cirque Napoleon Rancy's three-week stand in Marseilles, Manya and I walked from the circus to our hotel, with Lottie and Prinz following us, as usual. Just as we were approaching the hotel entrance, I heard a piercing yelp, and, turning around, beheld the big, hulking brick mason in the act of grabbing Lottie and making off with her.

At almost the same moment, however, the slippery, frantically squirming little Lottie wriggled out of the man's grasp and dashed after Manya into the hotel. Six or seven rough-looking men were standing on the sidewalk nearby at the time and one of them spoke up.

"Say, Mister, why don't you and your friend go after that fellow? He tried to steal your dog, didn't he!"

My friend was a fellow *artiste* in the circus, who had joined us on our walk to the hotel, and he and I proceeded to do exactly what this man on the sidewalk suggested. We caught up with the man, too—with the thieving, big brick mason, that is—up a dark, narrow street not far from there. I put an arm twist on him, and my friend gave him a smash in the face. So far, so good, it was, but not for long, because we were quickly descended upon by the six interlopers we had just passed, all of them brandishing clubs.

Fortunately, I was taking Manya's electric flat-iron back to the hotel from the circus and had it in my hand. The flat-iron had an electric cord permanently attached to it, which enabled me to use the iron as a swinging flail. The fact that I was a well-conditioned bareback rider, much in prime, stood me in good stead in the battle that now took place, and I flailed that flat-iron indiscriminately and with all the fury I could summon at what seemed like an avalanche of bodies and clubs. My companion from the circus, an acrobat and trapezist, was as deft and agile as a cat and had muscular strength that could bend rods, if need be. He was not the kind to seek a fight, but he was the last to avoid one when it came his way. He took care of at least three of our assailants that night, and he did so in a hurry. Meanwhile, my flat-iron had had a discouraging effect on the rest of the brick mason's friends, who retreated before the whirling iron and disappeared in the darkness.

At this juncture I heard someone moaning, as if in pain, and soon traced the sound to my friend, who was lying on the street at the curb. He had a deep scalp wound from a club, or maybe a brick. I picked him up and started carrying him in the direc-

tion of the hotel, but ran into a *gendarme,* who escorted us to a
hospital, where my friend had his wound sewed up and band-
aged. When that had been done, we returned to the scene of
combat with two *gendarmes* and from there went into the nearby neighborhood in which the brick mason and his supporters
were known to hang out. Presently, the tall and broad-shoul-
dered figure of the man we were looking for emerged from an
alleyway.

"There is the man," I said, my friend concurring in the iden-
tification, whereupon the gendarmes stopped him and took him
into custody.

The would-be kidnaper of Lottie, from whom I had snatched
Prinz, had a pair of black eyes and several badly swollen contu-
sions on the face, along with some broken teeth. We filed charges
against him that night and had him put in jail. Later on that
same night, while en route to the next stop in the Cirque Napoleon Rancy, I became aware of a number of bruises and con-
tusions myself. However, when we came back to Marseilles in
the following years, there was no sign of the brick mason, and
Lottie and Prinz were unmolested.

The Bears: Topsy, Jimmy, Darling, Teddy, and Pete

Not long after coming to France from Italy in 1921, I bought
five bear cubs from a band of gypsies, named them Topsy,
Jimmy, Darling, Teddy, and Pete and began training them. To
train a full-grown bear is too difficult to be practicable, and well-
trained grown bears are hard to come by. It is best, therefore,
to procure bears at the cub stage if the purpose is to make performers out of them.

Two of my cubs were Siberian silver grays, a variety of the
Euro-Asiatic bear. Two were dark brown and not unlike the
grizzlies of North America. One was a silver-tipped specimen of
similar kind. All grew to large size, the Siberian to a height of
eight feet when standing.

A bear is first trained to sit and stand on a pedestal, to which he is chained, and he is taught to stand up and hold his position when off the pedestal during the act. A bear can strike with his forepaws when standing, of course, but has less maneuverability in that position than when on all fours, so that any disposition to attack can be better apprehended.

In my act with the bears I had two dancing pairs and a bear that did a solo act. This solo dancer held a bottle in his paws and drank from it as he danced, which he enjoyed doing, for the reason that the bottle contained sugared water. Finally, this bear flopped over on his back while continuing to hold the bottle and to drink from it. When the bottle was taken from him, he got up and, in the manner of one who has had too much of something far stronger than sugared water, staggered from the ring.

My bears all rode bicycles and scooters, performed on roller skates, did headstands, and so on, and Jimmy, the silver-tipped gray, learned to make a forward somersault from a springboard.

Bears have certain traits in common, but they have their own individualities, and differ from one another in terms of disposition and amenability to training, etc. That they are uniquely comical and always amusing is well known. The fact remains, however, that they are wild animals and must at all times be regarded as such.

Bears are cunning. When in the mood to attack, they wait for that first moment when the trainer is not looking. Topsy, one of my big Siberians, was extremely mean. Since he had attacked me on numerous occasions, I had to keep a close and wary eye on him. One day in Portugal in 1929, during a rehearsal, he tried it again, this time as he was getting down from his pedestal on command. Within a split second after putting his forepaws down on the floor, he snapped at me with lightning suddenness and tore a sizeable piece of flesh out of my left thigh and a mouthful of material from my heavy breeches and underclothing. It could not be said that Topsy attacked me while I was unaware, because I had observed a tell tale gleam in his eyes and knew what he was of a mind to attempt. It was the suddenness of the bite, rather, at this juncture, that surprised.

After that successful bite and a taste of human blood, my big, bad Siberian bear became meaner and more treacherous than ever. He was so given to biting without provocation, thereafter, that he became dangerous even in his cage. Consequently, I had a special cage made for him, in which the bars were so close together that the hand of a child could be inserted between them only with difficulty.

While working in the circus in Albacete, Spain, with the Albanos, the famous troupe of clowns, I saw one of the Albanos put his finger between the bars of this cage to touch my mean Siberian's nose. I warned him agaiat this practice, but there came a day, nevertheless, when he did it again. I was informed of this fact by an outcry of pain coming from the direction of Topsy's cage. My big, bad Siberian had bitten off the end of Mr. Albanos' finger.

One morning in the Cirque Rancy in France, Darling, one of the best of my performing brown bears, was so profoundly asleep in his cage that he couldn't be awakened. Alarmed, I summoned the veterinarian, who, on examining the bear, found his pulse and temperature normal and nothing apparently wrong with him other than the very deep sleep. Not until 48 hours had passed were we able to rouse him, and even then he was so unsteady on his paws that he could not take part in the performance for another day. In the meantime, a careful investigation revealed the cause of the sleep. As they finally admitted, the keepers had filled one of the feed buckets with wine they had brought into the circus for their own consumption, and had left the bucket on the floor at a point along the route the bears followed as they were being returned to their cages from the ring after their act. Darling had come upon that bucket and before the keepers discovered him in the act had drained it of its intoxicating contents.

During the five years between our arrival in Paris from Italy in the fall of 1921 and our going to Spain in 1926, we did well, through long and continuous work, toward recouping the losses sustained before that. But we made the mistake of sending our earnings to the German, Austrian, and Hungarian banks. The collapse of the currencies in those countries, through inflation, left us not a great deal better off financially than we were on our arrival in France in 1921. In this connection, I remember a letter from our bank in Budapest in which an officer of the institution expressed regret at having to inform us that inflation had canceled out what we had there. There was nothing funny about that, needless to say, yet I laughed out loud when I read the letter. Mme. Rancy, who was standing nearby at the time, turned to me and asked: "And what is so amusing, Arthur?"

When I read the letter to her, translating it into French as I read it, she exclaimed commiseratingly:

"Oh, Arthur, I am so sorry to hear that. But how can you laugh about it? I am afraid I would feel like killing myself."

VII

Iberia

A Serio-Comic Bareback Act in Barcelona

ON CONCLUDING an engagement in the Cirque d'Hiver, Paris, in November, 1926, we put our old bareback horses Boyar and Romeo, the Arabian high-school horse Zebridge, and five performing bears on the train and took them with us across the Pyrenees to Barcelona.

This was the beginning of a long sojourn in Spain and Portugal, during which we were to become well acquainted with both. Though we were in those two countries in times of unrest, and passed through more violent episodes than there are fingers on one hand, we were received with hospitality, became fluent in the languages, and made many friends.

Spain and Portugal are like no other lands. They have cultural affinities, but each has its own amalgam of flavors and diversities and an identity that cannot be confused with the other.

69

In Barcelona, in the Circo Olympia, in the time of Gen. Miguel Primo de Rivera, I made my act with the bears, Manya rode the high-school, and we worked together in a serio-comic bareback act we had evolved in France. This act, billed as "Miss Marietta," had been a great success in France and other European countries, but we were newcomers in Spain and could only hope that it would be as well liked there. Manya made her entry in this act on the back of the snow-white Boyar, and was introduced as the celebrated equestrienne, "Miss Marietta." Wearing the black suit of a Spaniard of the better status for an evening occasion, I took a seat unobtrusively in one of the boxes, but began soon to draw attention to myself by giving vent to a vociferous and uninhibited admiration for the stunning ballerina on the white horse. My shrill whistles and exclamations of approval brought unrestrained but visible manifestations of annoyance among the onlookers, and it was not long before there were cries of "Shut up!" and "Throw him out!" This only encouraged me, of course, and when the *policia* strode gravely on to the scene, to prevent violence and to take me into custody, I mounted the railing in front of me, jumped into the ring, and ran after the object of my admiration. With the *policia* in pursuit, I jumped again, this time from the ground on to the rump of the galloping Boyar. The indignation of the spectators now gave way to astonishment, then to applause, as "Miss Marietta" smilingly acquiesced in my intrusion and the fact became clear that I, too, was a bareback rider.

There were risks in this role, and I did not always come away unpummeled before jumping into the ring beyond the reach of my would-be assailants and the *policia*. The act was invariably, and even immensely, popular, however, so the risks were calculated.

State of Siege in Oporto

A booking for the month of January, 1927, in the Coliseu dos Recreios in Lisbon took us from Spain and initiated what was to be a memorable four years in Portugal. In the meantime, we had accepted a contract to work in combination with another circus in the Palacio de Cristal, Oporto, and the first week in February found us there, in that teeming, terraced city on the north bank of the Douro. The Palacio de Cristal, a huge glass and iron structure, which is not unlike London's Crystal Palace, is at the western extremity of the city, overlooking the gorge of the Douro. We had been unable to find suitable living quarters near the circus, and the hotel in which we did find domicile was a good two miles away.

One of the people with acts in the circus was a lion trainer of French nationality by the Russian name of Ivanoff. This man was a spectacular showman and a fine animal trainer, and the display of an awesome jungle ferocity on the part of his lions never failed to thrill the spectators.

One of his lions, a magnificent specimen, was the huge and luxuriantly maned D'Artagnan. This old lion eclipsed all others in his display of truculence. He challenged his trainer again and again at every performance and gave every indication of an untamed and untamable savagery. But D'Artagnan was an actor, no more than that. In actuality, he was a great big, good-natured, lazy pet, excepting during the act, as was well evidenced on one occasion during the Oporto engagement when a drunken keeper turned up lying dead to the world beside the old lion and right up against him in his cage. D'Artagnan was sleeping peacefully.

With the rest of Ivanoff's lions, three full grown lionesses and one other male, also full grown, it was quite otherwise, yet it was around D'Artagnan the actor that Ivanoff had built his act.

One night in February we were awakened in our hotel by the sound of gunfire and the *rat-a-tat-tat-tat* of machine guns, and were even more startled a few moments later by a detonation of such violence that the building trembled as though it was being shaken by an earthquake. As we were soon to find out, an army uprising against the regime of Gen. Antonio Carmona, which became a bloody insurrection, was beginning. The insurrectionists had seized control of Oporto, and their positions were being shelled by Carmona's batteries from outside the city. A state of siege had been declared and was made known to us by rebel soldiers, who came into the hotel and apprised us of an order to the civilian population to remain indoors and in basements for the duration of the siege.

No one in his right mind would have had any inclination to disobey this order, but compliance with it did not relieve us of fears for the safety of our animals two miles away at the Palacio de Cristal. Our first fear was of the bombardment from the seaward side, but there was nothing we could do about that. There was another fear. The supply of grain for the horses would soon be running out. Milk, which was fed with cooked rice to the bears, would be needed. How long would the siege last? No one knew. Meanwhile, to the west of us, under the same roof with our horses, were Ivanoff's lions, D'Artagnan and the others. Big cats must have meat—raw meat—and when they don't get it, they become rampant. In the knowledge that his keepers were not likely to take the risk of going out of the circus to get the meat, even if permitted to, Ivanoff was desperate. The lions would already be hungry and pacing back and forth in their cages. Soon they would be lashing at the bars and one or more of them might break out. We thought of our horses.

In our anxiety over this prospect, we informed a rebel officer of our predicament and were stopped short with the suggestion that the lions be shot. With that poor Ivanoff went wild. He was an eloquent man in his way, in gesture and by way of facial expression, if not in the use of the Portuguese tongue. What? Shoot the wonderful D'Artagnan and the rest of his performing lions. No! No! No! No! Why, they were his bread and butter, his very life! If they were shot, he would be ruined. He would commit suicide. What he was able to do with these lions was the product of a skill he had worked for a lifetime to develop. And as for D'Artagnan, he was without equal. There would never be another like him. Ivanoff groaned, and looked as though he was about to faint. The young officer was impressed.

In the meantime, information had come to us that a number
of cavalry horses, which had been killed in the fighting, were
lying dead in the streets in the vicinity of the Palacio de Cristal,
and that gave us the idea of going across town to get some of
that horse meat to the lions. Not until the third day of the siege
was our request for such permission granted, however. We
would be permitted to go during the daylight hours and would
have to negotiate the distance on our own. If we were to appear
on the streets during the night, we were told, we would be shot
at on sight. Gen. Carmona's troops, preparing to retake the city
from the rebels, were fighting their way into the environs at
several points as our permission came through. Many of the
streets had been barricaded and blocked off, and some were no
safer than a rifle range during target practice. We did not relish
the journey. But we had too much at stake not to attempt it.

Emerging from the hotel at daybreak, to the accompaniment
of machine gun and rifle fire, which seemed close at hand, we
made our way westward by back-alley and across-block, now
crawling on all fours, now making a dash to cover and waiting,
only to proceed again, hugging the walls of the buildings as we
went, from street to street, with the bark of artillery pieces and
the all-too-near explosion of shells in our ear drums.

Pressing on through the narrow and irregular granite streets
of old Oporto, dark, deserted and cavernous between rows of
storied, balconied buildings, we came at last into an area, west
and north of the city, where we managed to rent a yoke of big,
brown, long-horned oxen and a stone drag of an ancient kind.
With this equipment we picked up several of the dead horses,
dragged them to the circus, and fed big chunks of the raw meat
to the lions.

When we had first arrived at the Palacio de Cristal in the first
week of February, we had had the pick of the stabling facilities.
So we had quartered our horses apart from the other animals on
the well-ventilated side of the building, the one with large windows. Late in the afternoon of the day before the outbreak of
the insurrection, I had decided to switch my horses around to

the other side. That there had been unrest among the troops was known, but we had been given no grounds for anticipating anything like the events of the following night. Nevertheless, I had had a premonition. The ventilation on the side of the building to which we moved our horses was poor. But something had impelled me to make the move. And had this not been done, the horses would all have been killed, because the original quarters we had chosen were raked with shell fire.

As it was, we found our horses unscathed, if not too well-fed, The supply of hay at the stable had been ample, but there had been no grain for several days.

As we had feared, the hunger-crazed lions had been lashing at the sides of their cages, several of which the keepers had re-enforced with planks and girdled with chains.

We also found some very hungry bears at the circus. Dry loaves of bread, an accustomed part of their diet, could have been obtained in the neighborhood, but the keepers had feared to go out after them. A supply of rice for them was in the wagons, but there was no milk in which to mix the rice. We therefore boiled it in water and added sugar. Meat, I should add, is not fed to performing bears, because it makes them ill-tempered, and an ill-tempered bear is a bad risk.

Within the next day or so, Gen. Carmona's forces regained possession of the city.

Casualties had been heavy, and damage from shells and rifle fire considerable. With the lifting of the siege, Manya and Dorita, who had come out to the circus, went down to the park below the Palacio de Cristal but, on observing what was going on down there, came back quickly.

Soldiers, municipal workers, and volunteers were picking up the bodies of the slain and loading them into wagons. Some were engaged in scraping dried blood and gore from the mosaic walks, which they then hosed down. It was there that some of the fiercest hand-to-hand fighting of the insurrection had occurred.

With order again established, the busy people of Oporto returned quickly to their activities; the barges, steamers, and picturesque sailing craft reappeared on the Douro, and Portugal's second city was its noisy self again.

A week later we set up headquarters in a suburb and began the organization of a new and larger circus, in preparation for a tour of the country in combination with the Circo Mariano. Our own circus, the American Show-El Grande Circo Ecuestre, now came into being.

Expeditions to the Azores and Madeira

Two brightly intervening episodes of our four-year sojourn in Portugal were the expeditions we made in the autumn of 1928 and again in 1929 to the Azores and Madeira with a company of 60 people, 40 horses, our performing bears, and a variety of supporting acts.

So successful was the journey into the Atlantic in 1928 and so pleasant the whole experience that we repeated it the following year, and would have gone back again had it been feasible. Our itinerary in the Azores consumed six weeks, with stops at Horta, on the island of Fayal; Ponta Delgado on Sao Miguel, where we worked in the Coliseu Avenida, and Angra do Hero-isimo, on Terceira.

An unusual sight that greeted us on our first day at Angra, one that could be witnessed there on every working day, was that of the basket-carrying dogs of Terceira. It was a few minutes before the noon hour when dogs by the dozens began coming out of the houses and other dwelling places carrying baskets, which they gripped in their jaws by the handles. They were taking lunch to their masters, at work in the neighboring wheat fields and gardens or tending sheep and cattle in pasture. Looking very business-like as they trotted down the walks into and along the byways toward their destinations, each one independently bent on his mission, the dogs paid no attention to each other or to the people they passed. Later on they reappeared, going home with the empty baskets.

It was at Angra do Heroisimo that I bought the fine gray
stallion Canario to take back to Portugal for development as a
high-school horse.

From the flowered and unspoiled Azores in the middle of
the Atlantic we sailed to Funchal, on the island of Madeira, a
mountain in the ocean, crowned with rock gardens. There, as in
the Azores, the warm-hearted hospitality of the people and the
generosity of their response to our efforts made us feel as though
we belonged there and were of them.

The 'Bull Horses' of the Tourado

The breed of riding horses of which the Portuguese are
rightfully proud is exemplified in its highest and most characteristic form by the handsome and wonderfully-trained horses
of the bull ring. In the *tourado,* the Portuguese equivalent of
corrida in Spain, the *festa brava,* as it is popularly known, the
more ancient practice of fighting the bulls from horseback, is
adhered to. And nowhere in the world today is a more conclusive demonstration of art in the training and management
of the horse to be seen. Significantly, the schooling and development of the horse for this demanding and dangerous role is a
practical application of the principles and the method of the
high-school. The "bull-horses" of the *tourado* are high-schooled.
But they are high-schooled and developed for combat, which
makes them unique in the present day.

The horses of this excellent breed are raised in Portugal in the
provinces of Ribatejo and Alemtejo, or beyond the Spanish
border in Andalusia, and are substantially the same as the Andalusian horses of Spain. Like his counterpart, the Andalusian,
the Portuguese horse is of ancient lineage, and, though lighter
than the ancestral type, reflects his descent from the more massive, and more Roman-nosed horses of the 17th century. There
is still the tendency to the Roman nose, more so in some strains
than in others, but the characteristic is less pronounced. Typically, a good specimen is short in the back and cannon bones,

long in the forearms, in the underline, and from hips to the hocks. The shoulders should be deep, powerful, and well laid back, the quarters massive without heaviness. Fine natural action, a proud bearing, elasticity, and great freedom in the shoulders are marks of the breed. Many of the best individuals are gray.

In the past, the objective of the *cavaleiro*, as the mounted bull-fighter is called in Portugal, was the killing of the bull, and the kill was administered, as it is by the bull-fighters on foot in Spain, with a *rejon*, or sword. Today the killing of the bull is prohibited in Portugal, so the sword has been dispensed with there. In the *festa brava*, accordingly, there is no "moment of truth." The role of Portugal's mounted bull-fighters may be a less dramatic one than that of the matador in the Spanish *corrida*, but it is not less impressive. What the *cavaleiro* has to do is to evade the bull's charges by outmaneuvering the beast and to immobilize his fighting effectiveness by thrusting metal-pointed, long wooden sticks into his shoulders and back. These sticks are thin, and they are made so that they will break at about a quarter of their length, the arrow-like metal points remaining in the bull's hide. As a conclusive demonstration of dexterity and daring, as well as of horsemanship, in thrusting such darts into the bull, the *cavaleiro*, sometimes on the requests of the more demanding of the *aficionados*, will resort to the use of darts on very short sticks, which increases the difficulty of implanting the darts at the right places on the bull's neck and shoulders. After the *cavaleiro* has succeeded in demonstrating the superiority of mount and man over his bovine adversary, he retires from the scene of combat in favor of the *forcados*, or the bull-fighters on foot. The function of the *forcados* is to capture the bull. One of them advances, inviting a charge, and when the bull comes at him, he opens his arms and at the right moment closes them around the animal's neck. The purpose is to hold on to the bull's head in an effort to bring him to a stand, a feat, which, in the accomplishment, calls for skill and courage. When it has been done, the rest of the *forcados* rush in and in combination bring the tired but still dangerous bull under control.

In Portugal's bull rings the bulls are *embolacao,* which means that they have their horns sheathed in leather and the points padded. The danger of mortal injury to horse and rider is thus reduced, though it is by no means eliminated. And in Portugal the bulls are generally bigger and proportionately more powerful than all except the largest bulls of the Spanish *corrida.* I became acquainted with some of the leading *cavaleiros* of that period and well acquainted with the great Manuel Casimiro de Almeida, who honored us on one occasion with a demonstration of his horsemanship in our own circus.

Bullfighting from the back of a high-schooled horse has been on the increase in Spain in recent years, but the bulls are fought *en puntas,* or with the horns unsheathed. Not to be outdone by their Spanish neighbors, the leading Portuguese *cavaleiros,* such as Senhor Joao Branco Nuncio and Senhor Simao de Veiga, give the Spaniards a taste of the Portuguese brand of bullfighting in the bull rings of Madrid, Seville, and Barcelona, where they fight the biggest and most formidable bulls in all Spain from the backs of their marvelously-trained and very valuable horses. This they do *en puntas,* killing the bull in the Spanish manner with the sword. Bullfighting from horseback in Spain is called *Suerte de Rejonear,* and the Spanish equivalent of Portugal's *cavaleiro tourero* is a *rejoneador.* The Senores Don Alvaro Domecq and Antonio Canero were the outstanding exponents of this art in the recent past in Spain. The Peruvian Senorita Conchita Cintron and the Duque de Pinohermoso followed them. Angel Peralta is the most acclaimed of the *rejoneadores* today.

VIII

Fantasia Ecuestre Portuguesa

Senhor Arturo of Lisboa

IN THE SUMMER of 1927, in Portugal, I had bought Sultan, a
gray Portuguese stallion of outstanding natural brilliance, before my purchase in the following year, at Angra do Heroisimo,
in the Azores of the Portuguese-bred Canario. These two horses,
especially Sultan, were an answer to the high-school rider's
dreams, and yet, just as they were coming into their potential
I sold them. It came about in this way.

On returning to Portugal from our second expedition to the
Azores and Madeira, I wrote letters to the directors of the
leading circuses, variety theatres, and music halls of Europe,
telling them about my high-school act and announcing my
availability as a high-school exhibitionist. Most of these men I
knew, or had known, and they, in turn, were acquainted with
the Konyot name, but in association most prominently with

79

bareback riding. When the weeks passed and I received not one single answer to my solicitations, the fact was brought home to me that Arthur Konyot, well known as a bareback rider, was not being taken seriously, and was not going to be, when he represented himself as a high-school rider. The suggestion was clear. I would have to become someone else. And that someone, I decided, would be "Senhor Arturo, the Noted Portuguese High-School Rider," my new alter ego. Exit Arthur Konyot, into the shadows! Enter "Senhor Arturo!"

The first thing I did in my new identity was to compose a letter. I took great pains with it and had it transcribed into Portuguese. Why not? Was I not a Portuguese? This letter I sent to but one prospect—the Zirkus Hagenbeck in Berlin. If I could obtain a contract to exhibit there, I reasoned, my act would be seen by the most important directors of circus and stage in the whole of Europe. My own ability as a trainer and exhibitionist would have to do the rest.

Did I get an answer to this letter, which was my second to the Zirkus Hagenbeck, but my first under the name of "Senhor Arturo?" I did. And I got it within a week. It contained a full acceptance of the conditions I had stipulated and a contract, which was signed by Heinrich Hagenbeck, to make my act in the Zirkus Hagenbeck in Berlin through a period of two months, beginning on the first day in February and ending on the last day in March, 1930. I had written, in the meantime, to my brother Adolph, who was equestrian director at that time in the very circus I hoped to be working in, and introduced him to "the great Senhor Arturo." He would have to play along with me in my new role, I said, and be prepared to greet "a distinguished high-school rider from Lisboa!"

In better than due course, about 10 days ahead of time, that is, appropriately attired in the habiliments of a Portuguese *cavaleiro*, nothing overlooked, I boarded ship with Sultan and Canario at the docks in Lisbon and set sail for the port of Hamburg, home city of the Hagenbeck dynasty of zoo curators, animal trainers, and circus proprietors. Before taking my depar-

ture, I telegraphed the director of the circus to let him know
the steamer I was coming on and the scheduled time of its
arrival. We had a good voyage, and when I disembarked at
Cuxhaven, the port of Hamburg, I was met at the dock by none
other than Heinrich Hagenbeck himself, the proprietor. In
truth, though I had not seen Herr Hagenbeck for a number of
years, I recognized him, but gave no such indication as he approached and addressed me.

"Are you Senhor Arturo?", he asked, though he probably had
little doubt about it, as he beheld me in the get-up that strongly
indicated it. I responded affirmatively with an off-pitch, "Ya."
The two grooms Herr Hagenbeck brought with him were sent
into the ship after Sultan and Canario. I went along to direct
them, and within a few minutes my well-bandaged, richly-
haltered, blanketed, and hooded Portuguese horses appeared
coming down the gangplank, led by the uniformed grooms, who
loaded them with an experienced hand into the truck that was
there to take them to the Hagenbeck Zoo in nearby Stellingen.
There they were to be quartered overnight, and then shipped
to Berlin in the morning. Herr Hagenbeck's chauffeur and an
attendant put my luggage in the proprietor's limousine, and
we motored swiftly out to the stables at Stellingen and from
there to my hotel, where we parted.

While en route to Stellingen, I studiously affected only a
meager knowledge of the German language, and felt that I was
being successful in doing so. Presently, Herr Hagenbeck spoke
up.

"Somehow, Senhor Arturo, I have the feeling that I have seen
you before. Where could that have been?"

"In Spain or Portugal, perhaps, but not in Germany," I replied, in my labored German, and added: "I am for always in
Portugal been. In Spain, yes. Other place, no."

At an early hour the next morning my horses were trucked to
the train and they were already in their car, with a groom in at-
tendance, when I arrived at the station. "Senhor Arturo" had
not been long seated in his first-class compartment when there

was a shrill whistle up ahead. We were off on the first fast express of the day for Berlin. After being deposited at my hotel the day before, I had wired Adolph the time of my arrival on the morrow. As the equestrian director, he would be getting that information anyway, I knew, but there could be no harm in his hearing from "Senhor Arturo" directly.

At the *bahnhof* (railroad station) in Berlin I did not have to look long for the familiar figure and features of my brother, from whom I had been separated for nine years. For at the very moment I stepped down on to the platform I heard the voice I knew as well as any in the world.

"Senhor Arturo, I presume."

Yes, it was Adolph, inimitably so, and no other. I turned around, and there he was. How wonderful it was to see him! Momentarily I forgot, but remembered in time. So did he. We had a role to play. The equestrian director of the Zirkus Hagenbeck held up his end, performing faultlessly. And "Senhor Arturo, the famous high-school rider from Lisboa," followed through. A strict adherence to the formality that was advisable, in the circumstances, did not prevent us from exchanging a few thoughts and sentiments *sotto voce*, however.

"Arthur," said Adolph, beneath his breath, "you are more Portuguese than Portugal. I'm impressed."

I had a week to put in before beginning my engagement in the Zirkus Hagenbeck, and, with my horses quartered at a fashionable riding academy off the Linden at the Brandenburger Tor, was ideally situated to employ the time to advantage. The riding academy was a school in which the principles of equitation were taught to a nicety. Its stabling facilities were excellent and the feature of it, from my point of view, was the large riding hall, in which I could exercise, and had already begun exercising, my horses. The high-school rider from Portugal and his Portuguese horses were attracting attention. Those who had been watching them were impressed, and among them was Herr Kock, the Direktor and Reitmeister, who came to me and said:

"Senhor Arturo, I am going to ask a favor of you. Tomorrow

we are being honored. Commissionsrat Albert Schumann, the celebrated master of the *haute école,* of whom, no doubt, you have heard, has consented to ride the high-school at our Sunday morning *manoeuvre* and *quadrille.* We would be additionally honored if you would be so kind as to present your horses at the same time." I replied that it would be a pleasure, but that I was under contract with the Zirkus Hagenbeck and would have to obtain Herr Hagenbeck's permission.

"Ah, yes," said Reitmeister Kock. "The Messrs. Hagenbeck, Heinrich, and Lorenz. Excellent gentlemen, both of them, and friends of mine. Will you make that request of them? I will ask them, too." I knew, of course, that those Sunday musical rides were dress affairs, so, in the labored German, from which I had not deviated, I said:

"Herr Direktor, there is a difficulty. I do not have with me the top hat and habit for so important an occasion, only what is correct in my own country." Herr Kock hastened to reassure me.

"My dear Senhor, that is a matter of no consequence."

A glint of amusement now came into his eyes, and, lowering his voice, as if to impart a confidence, he said: "We are envious of you as you are."

Consider my appointments. I wore a wide-brimmed black Portuguese hat, which was similar to the Spanish *Cordoban,* and had grown rather extravagant but neatly barbered sideburns. My well-tailored, silver-embroidered, black-braided gray jacket was strictly Portuguese, my black riding breeches and boots the same. For formal occasions and street wear I donned a dark gray cape with a red silk lining which accented the ensemble. Is it any wonder that I became the object of more attention thus attired than I would have been receiving in my true identity, as that more prosaic figure, Arthur Konyot? I spent my first evening in Berlin with Adolph and Lilly in their apartment. On seeing me for the first time in this splendor, as "the great so and so from Lisboa," in which terms Adolph, in high humor, announced my entry, Lilly exclaimed:

"Why, Arthur, I never saw you look so dashing. You are even rakish. It is terrific. Has not Manya said the same?"

"Do you know what Manya said?" I interjected. "She said I had better keep this outfit well brushed and free of all spots or the effect will be ruined." I had already wired Manya to join me in Berlin, which she did, a few weeks later.

Sultan the Magnificent

On Sunday morning an automobile was sent to my hotel at 7:30 to convey me to the riding academy for the opening at 8, at which time Commissionsrat Schumann and "Senhor Arturo" were to exhibit. I had chosen to be 10 minutes late, but no later, so I did not come down to the waiting automobile until 10 minutes had elapsed. Upon being whisked over to the riding academy, I went directly to the stables and there found Sultan and Canario saddled, bridled, and groomed to a gleaming. After checking the bridle, the bits, reins, stirrups, and girthing, I mounted Sultan and proceeded to the gate. The gate opened and the sight I then beheld has been anything but forgotten to this day. One hudred splendidly mounted, formally attired riders, both men and women, the women in side saddles, lined the great hall for its entire circumference, the horses against the wall and facing the ring. Commissionsrat Albert Schumann was waiting on his horse close to the entrance at one side. As the gate swung wide, a 50-piece band opened up with a Portuguese *pasodoble,* or two-step march. I entered on Sultan.

Sultan was not a particularly impressive individual as he stood, but he was an equine ballerina when in motion. No other horse that I have owned, had anything to do with, or seen, with one possible exception, could perform so many of the "airs" of the high-school with such elevation and abounding grace. Nevertheless, in his execution of that *piece de resistance* of them all, the *passage,* he was in a period of intermittency, and had been for a month or more. Though he was capable of a *passage* that had held people spellbound, and would be doing it again,

I could not take a chance with him at that movement before so
exacting and elect an audience, and had decided, accordingly,
to make an entry at a collected trot. This was an electric moment for both horse and rider, and Sultan the magnificent became a medium for the charge. What happened as we entered
the riding hall was by no means a miracle, but it was thrillingly
gratifying to me, the trainer of this horse and his rider, with so
much at stake, and fortuitous in high degree. I said I had decided to make my entry at a collected trot, and so I had. But
something happened to Sultan as we took off, and it could not
have happened at a better calculated moment. Wide-eyed and
surcharged, with his nostrils distended, as though he was about
to neigh in joyous excitement, Sultan perceived his surround-
ings. I felt him under me. I felt his springs, and knew, of course,
at the instant he began to do it just what he was going to do.
Sultan, my Sultan, responding ecstatically to the stimulus of the
occasion, and beginning it practically from the stand, came
soaring into the riding hall at the *passage!* At an almost unbe-
lievably altitudinous, beautifully accented, all-on-springs *passage!* Which he sustained, with not the slightest diminution in
the rapture of it until his rider conveyed the instruction to him,
"That's enough."

This was only the beginning of a memorable exhibition. But
what a beginning! Commissionsrat Schumann worked on one
side of the hall, and gave a letter-perfect demonstration of the
art he had practiced for so long. "Senhor Arturo" worked on the
other side. The applause was ovational. Along with Commissionsrat Schumann on his Holsteiner, I rode Sultan to an encore,
and responded to a second encore on Canario. In seats overlooking the hall were Adolph and Lilly and the Messrs. Heinrich
and Lorenz Hagenbeck, accompanied by the great animal
trainer, Richard Sawade, who was the director of the Zirkus
Hagenbeck. Among the first to offer his congratulations was the
elder of the two Hagenbecks.

"Senhor Arturo, you rode magnificently," he said, extending
his hand. "That horse would make you famous, if you were not

already famous." Thereupon, he changed the theme of his remarks and repeated what he had said in his automobile in Hamburg.

"I still have the feeling, Senhor, that I have seen you before."

I replied with a gesture indicating "perhaps," and reiterated my retort of the previous occasion: "In Portugal, maybe, or Spain. It is possible."

That Sultan had reached the pinnacle of brilliance that day was made clear not only by the applauce and a standing ovation during the exhibition, but by the extravagantly complimentary remarks that were communicated to me afterward. In a more concrete way, the fact was attested to by the number of offers I had for the horse, all of which I turned down with the statement, "Not for sale."

The scene now changed to the Zirkus Busch, where the Hagenbecks were giving guest performances. The name of Hagenbeck is synonymous the world over with animals and animal acts. Some of the best animal acts to be seen anywhere were on the program that year, and the animals appearing in them were referred to in the *Berliner Borsen Courier* of Feb. 4, 1930, as "the magnificent material, which is the strength and beauty of the Zirkus Hagenbeck."

Featured were Rudolph Matthies and his 15 Bengal tigers, Gustave Hundriesser with his elephants, Capt. Decker with his juggling walruses and sea lions, and an act with zebus, water-buffalo, and a jumping elk. Still, the horses were "the real sovereigns" in the Zirkus Hagenbeck that year, according to *Die Welt Am Abend* of Berlin (Feb. 4, 1930). This reference was to the eight Lipizzaners and the 22 Trakehners which Lulu Gautier presented at liberty; the horses of the *parforce* riders Elvie, Dolinda, and Kate, and the high-school horses of Albert Jeserich and "Senhor Arturo."

So decisively had Sultan retured to form at the *passage* in his exhibition in the riding academy that he forgot all about whatever it was that had been bothering him and excelled again in that "air," as in the other "airs" of the high-school, throughout the Hagenbeck engagement. People who had seen him in the riding academy came to see him in the circus, and some were so spellbound by the brilliance of his soaring grace that they came to see him not just once, but three and four times.

One night during the second week of my triumphant sojourn in Berlin as "Senhor Arturo" I had to confess my true identity to Heinrich Hagenbeck, who overheard me speaking a fluent German in conversation with a group of fellow *artistes*. It happened in the circus restaurant, where I was so busy eating and talking that I failed to observe Herr Hagenbeck as he came in and sat down at another table.

"Pardon my intrusion, Arthur Konyot, and all you fine people," he said, as he came over to our table and stood before us. "I knew I had seen you before Konyot." He looked directly at me. "Well, it was a good disguise, an effective role, I must say. You are a good actor, Konyot, and your brother covered you well."

He then gave me a good natured poke on the shoulder, and, in departing said: "Good evening, high-school rider, you rascal. Good evening, all of you."

A few days after the termination of my contract with the Hagenbecks, a young man who looked like a matinee idol came to me and asked what I wanted for Sultan. I told him, as I had told others, that the horse was not for sale. This did not discourage him, however; he returned every day and got the same answer. Still undismayed, on the last night he followed me to the stables after my act, and said: "Can't you put a price on him, Senhor Arturo? No harm in that."

I decided to have done with the man by putting a prohibitive price on the horse, and that is what I thought I had done when I named it. But I was wrong.

"Sold!" came the retort.

Sultan had become the property of one Jose Moser of Berlin. I suffered mixed emotions, thereafter, the more so because I had already agreed to let Adolph have Canario, a beautiful horse, young, sound, talented, and on his way. I went back to Portugal richer than before, but without one of the greatest high-school horses by natural endowment that I ever laid a hand on.

Vulcan, Nobre, Luzero, Pinto Silgo, Immaculado and Pinto

Through my having obtained that contract with the Zirkus Hagenbeck, which resulted in the success I had in Berlin with Sultan and Canario, I made a reputation for myself to the north of the Pyrenees as a trainer and rider of high-school horses.

In the meantime, my son and daughter, Alexander and Dorita, were growing up and had developed into good riders. The time had come, therefore, for us to begin creating a family high-school act, and to procure horses for it that would make a harmonious picture as a foursome. With that much determined upon, I lost no time in going out on a series of horse-buying trips and came up with the gray stallions Vulcan, Nobre, Luzero, and Pinto Silgo, the bay gelding Immaculado, and the piebald Pinto, which was Dorita's first high-school horse. These were the horses we developed for our new act and rode to acclaim all over Europe in the 1930's.

Vulcan was a Portuguese horse of the Palha Blanco (white straw) strain and of a strikingly traditional type. I acquired him from the Conde de Fontalve. A powerful individual of exceptional inner fire, he had proven too mettlesome for his trainer and had apparently come in for some inept handling. That, no doubt, is the reason I was able to buy him; in short, he was a problem horse. It was a struggle to put a bridle on him; he wouldn't take the bit. He struggled against being girthed and became a wild horse when mounted. Here, indeed, was a horse with spirit, but he was a frightened horse. I worked hard, long, and patiently with him, and had some rough sessions. Finally, after some five or six weeks, I succeeded in calming him, so that he could be bridled without a fuss and would take the bit. And the day came when he stopped his antics at being girthed and saddled and mounted. Still he was not reconciled and, in a seemingly incurable state of agitation, pawed the earth. This, I confess, I lost patience with, and I would have sold Vulcan had it not been for Manya, who still admired him for his fire and beauty. She put her foot down on my letting him go, so I turned him over to her. Manya spent many hours just getting to know Vulcan. Not until she felt he had come to know her and liked her did she begin to ride him. Methodically, asking very little from him, seeking only to gain his confidence, she rode him for short periods every day. It began to look as though this sort of thing was going to go on forever, but Manya was pleased, because the horse was improving, she insisted, and would soon be settling down. The improvement now became visible. It was only gradual, but it continued, until one fine day what seemed a literal wonder came to pass. Vulcan changed his mind about the whole business and came submissively to hand. From there on, learning quickly now, he behaved like a gentleman, and in another eight months or so Manya was riding him in our new act. Later on she would be riding him to ovational applause and he would be acclaimed the most beautiful high-school horse in the world. A natural way with horses, a pair of feeling hands, patience, determination, and equestrian tact had won the day. We brought Vulcan to the United States in 1940, and he lived until he was 30.

The gray horse Nobre had been the mount of a young *cavaleiro tourero* in Portugal. The *cavaleiro* died of influenza, and his father, from whom I sought to buy the horse, was determined that no other *cavaleiro* would ever take the place of his dead son on the back of that horse, the two being inseparable in his mind, so far as the *tourada* was concerned. It was not until I had committed myself in writing never to sell the horse to a *cavaleiro* or to anyone who would permit him to be returned to the bull ring that the father consented to my having him. Nobre, which means "noble" in Portuguese, was aptly named. A handsome dappled gray, trained for combat in the bull ring, he developed into a brilliant and consistent high-school horse. He, too, came to the United States with us in 1940.

Immaculado was of the rare and valued Alter breed, a variety of the Andalusian deriving its name from the villages of Alter do Chao and Alter Pedroso, in the province of Alemtejo. He had a distinctly thoroughbred look about him and moved in long gliding strides. At the change of leads he was perfection itself. Manya rode this fine bay in a solo feature of our family high-school act. I bought Immaculado from a Portuguese army major, who had been using him as a tournament jumper and using him hard. We lost him in France shortly before coming to the United States.

Pinto Silgo, like Nobre, had been trained for the *tourado* and proved himself to be worth his weight in gold as a high-school horse. Luzero was a Spanish Andalusian and our only Spanish horse. In the company of our Portuguese horses he was with his own kind. I bought him in Spain.

Los Aseveros

For our new high-school act we took the Portuguese pseudonym of Asevera, and it was under that name that we were to achieve repeated triumphs in high-school riding and showmanship, with top billing in the leading circuses and variety theatres of Portugal, Spain, France, England, Germany, Austria, Belgium, Denmark, Sweden, Poland, and several other countries, from the early 1930's on up until the outbreak of the second World War.

We developed our new act, "Fantasia Ecuestre Portuguesa," during a tour of the country and introduced it, full blown, in Lisbon at the Coliseu dos Recreios.* Then, in January, 1931, after an absence of five years, we returned to Spain to fill an engagement in the Circo Price in Madrid.

Through the happenstance of bad timing, our return to Spain coincided with the last days of Alfonso XIII and the monarchy, and, as we soon learned, a revolution was in the brew. A year

---

* Coliseu dos Recreios, coliseum of recreation. A very large structure with a seating capacity of 8,000 Used by the circus for nine months of the year. The rest of the time it was an opera house.

had elapsed since the fall of the directorate and the dismissal of Primo de Rivera, premier and virtual dictator. The decline in the value of the *peseta* and an accompanying rise in the cost of living were continuing. Strikes, riots, and growing disorder marred the Spanish scene. Despite these deep-seated troubles, however, show business was being conducted as usual and not as yet with any appreciable lack of patrons. We who rode for a living and were making enough money to put some aside could not complain. Besides, Spain was a fascinating country.

Small traveling circuses, many of them little more than embellished side-shows, creep up and down the coastal regions and the more populous and fertile valleys of the Spanish peninsula. Since there are almost no large circuses (not more than one or two), it is a common practice in Spain, as in Portugal, for two or more of these small circuses to combine for joint performances. More often than not such performances are conducted in the *plazas de toros,* which are rented on a 50-50 basis. After all expenses have been met, the profits are divided on some prearranged basis. While in process of establishing our own circus, we made a number of such joint performances, in combination with the Circo Hervas, the Circo Olympic, and the Circo Luftman.

IX

Fantasia Ecuestre Espanola

March and Countermarch in Albacete

IN NO OTHER country are tradition, customs, and folklore such a vital force in the present as they are in Spain. This is to be seen in the fervent realism of the festivals, processions, and pilgrimages which are almost continuously occurring around the calendar, in village, town, city, and country district all over Spain. Practically every community has its *feria* or its *fiesta*, and at the larger and more important ones, in an atmosphere of abandon to gayety and holiday making, music, dancing, processions, and bullfights, the circus and circuses will be found. At this point my mind reverts to the first *fiesta* we went to with our circus. The scene was in Albacete, in southeastern Spain, in September, 1931.

93

Albacete, long known for its efficient daggers, is a picturesque old city on the road to the Mediterranean from Madrid.
We had come there for the *fiesta* and had been assigned to a
location at a dead-end of the avenue on which the side-shows,
various and sundry amusements and exhibitions, and two other
circuses were situated. Since we were newcomers, and because
there was no other location to be had anyway, there seemed
nothing we could do about it. Our better-situated competitors
were in a position to entice the patronage of the passing crowd
before the latter were within sight of us, and there was the rub!
In short, only the left-overs, most of them without money, were
finding their way to our location. And, finally, we could not
hope to vie with our rivals in their specialty, which was a well-
practiced and all too effective kind of barking. In short, what
we faced was the prospect of a lean gate and financial loss. But
to merely bemoan that prospect was not to alter it, so we put
heads together in an effort to think up some way in which to
make up for our disadvantages.

A parade was decided on as a likely means of capturing interest and drawing spectators, so, after obtaining permission to
conduct one, we hired a band to lead it, some pretty girls to
ride in open carriages and lend their charms, and some men,
seven or eight of them, whom we made up as clowns, giving
to each one a free ticket to the performance and a few *pesetas*.
Behind the band in our procession were our eye-filling horses,
ridden by Manya and others of the troupe. The men wore short-
jacketed Andalusian costumes and wide-brimmed *Cordoban*
hats. Two of the women were in white and wore white lace
mantillas over high combs. The others had on becoming round,
black hats, touched off with a rose behind the ear. But what is
a circus without the clowns? We had some good professional
clowns of our own, who outdid themselves in furtherance of
our ends by performing their antics and acrobatics along the
flanks of the moving column. The squad of free-loaders, who
looked like clowns, but didn't know what to do about it, made
their contribution by swelling our numbers and marching as a

group behind the horses. After them, in delightful contrast, came the girls, in vari-colored dresses, and as gay as the birds that sing, in the festooned open carriages of blue and red, *a la feria*. A man and a bear carried out the rear, both of them riding bicycles. I was the man.

With this cavalcade, in the twilight of the early evening, we paraded on the wide walks and avenues of the fair grounds to strains from Ruperto Chapi's "Zarzuela Punao de Rosas" and Pascual Marquina's "Espana Cani." The crowd, in joyful mood, followed us on the circuit, and continued following us as we reversed our direction and countermarched past the rival circuses, and beyond, to our dead-end location. Within 20 minutes our big tent was packed, and for the rest of the *fiesta* our act enjoyed full patronage.

Later on in the evening, after the last spectator had gone, and the circus had been put to bed, we decided to go to one of the open-air restaurants at the *fiesta*. The air was vibrant with *flamenco* music, with singing, hand-clapping, and the clicking of *castanets*, coming from the *casetas* on the avenue, where dancing was going on. From our table in the restaurant under the night sky, in an atmosphere of song and laughter, we listened to the haunting rhythms of the gypsy music, as played by a guitarist across the way, watched the play of colored lights on a fountain nearby, and partook of good sustenance. A spirit not of revelry, merely, but of joyousness spontaneously expressed pervaded the atmosphere, and, in responding to it, we felt we were making progress in getting to know Spain and the Spanish people. With a considerable degree of satisfaction, we could reflect on the events of a day's unfolding, which demonstrated that a good parade, serving well to marshal attention and to attract people, is good show business.

High-School Revue at the Bullfights

Highlighting our second visit to Spain were the occasions on which we were engaged to lead the entry parades and to present our high-school act as a curtain-raiser at the *corridas de toros,* or bullfights. The inclusion of our act within the dramatically formalized ritualism of the *corrida* was an honor, as well as an innovation, and even our horses seemed to appreciate it. Here, indeed, was a setting for his act that a high-school rider might dream about, but has not often been provided in this modern day.

The bullfighting season begins in March and ends in October, and the itinerary of our engagements covered the span of it, from Alicante in mid-March to Barcelona in October. We were in Madrid at the *plaza monumental* during the *fiesta* of San Isidro Labrador in May, in Granada and Toledo during the *fiesta* of Corpus Christi in June, and in Salamanca, the heart of the bull-breeding country, during the *fiesta mayor* in September. We were also in Ovieda, Guadalajara, and several other places.

The bullfighter's entry parade, the *paseillo,* is a glittering procession of the *matadors* and their *cuadrillas,* or groups of assistants, which signals the beginning of the *corrida.* Prior to it, the scene within the *plaza de los toros* is of an exuberant expectancy, tempered with suspense. As the time to begin the *corrida* draws near and the suspense heightens, the band picks up the mood of the spectators and keynotes it with the stirring marches and *pasodobles* of the bull ring.

The *Presidente* is now in his box, watch in hand, waiting, usually for the clock to strike six. The clock strikes, whereupon, to a fanfare of trumpets and drums, two men on horseback advance across the arena to the *Presidente's* box. They are the *alguaciles,* or municipal officers, who are to lead the *paseillo.* They salute and take a position at the head of the procession, now in formation on the opposite side of the ring. Therewith, the entire brilliant company, to the tune of a *pasodoble,* proceeds across the yellow sand to the *barrera,* the red wooden barrier surrounding the ring, and comes to a stop before the *Presidente's* box, the participants baring their heads in formal salute. The *paseillo* is now over, and the procession disperses, all of it but the *alguaciles,* who remain standing. At this juncture, the *Presidente* throws a key to one of the *alguaciles.* It is the key, though only a symbolical one, to the *toril,* the gate through which the bull will enter, and the *alguacile* rides over to the *toril* and hands it to an official posted there. The long-awaited moment has arrived. There is a trumpet blast. The bull is released, the "brave bull," and comes charging on to the scene of his impending death.

It was this ceremonial opening of the *corrida,* as described, in which we participated, my son Alexander and I assuming the role of the *alguaciles.* Thereafter, during an interval at the conclusion of the *paseillo* and before the entry of the bull, we put on our revue. From a position in front of and facing the *Presidente's* box, our four grays standing abreast, we backed up to the center of the ring, and began our performance, guiding and interweaving our horses in a series of integrated figures, to the changing cadences of the music. In bringing the act to a conclusion, we advanced from the center at the *passage* in unison and came to a halt, again in front of the *Presidente's* box, saluted, made a bow, and backed out, trotting backward to the exit.

Revolution in Spain

In the elections of April 12, 1931, the monarchist right was defeated, and two days later King Alfonso, for whom events had proved too big, sailed from Cartagena for France, never to return. Thereupon, the latent fires of Spanish extremism and anarchy broke into flame and produced the revolution of 1931. Radical demonstrations, strikes, street-fighting, and anti-clerical outrages were the order of the day; convents and churches were sacked and burned, with only limp interference from the police; and volunteers rose from the population to defend the clergy and the properties of the church. These were the birth pains of the Second Republic, which came into being in the wake of the elections for the Cortes Constituyentes late in June, 1931. If the creation of this new order of things was a step in the right direction, as many saw it and others hoped, the deep divisions and animosities that welled out from within in the civil strife of 1931 remained.

We were in Barcelona in the Circo Olympia in the months of January and February, 1932. Anarchist disorders, several of which occurred in January, were put down with violence by the Republican government. That summer we were on tour with the Circo Corzana, showing in the *plazas de los toros*. Pilaging mobs, spurred on by agitators, of which there was no lack, went about their business in defiance of the police. An unsuccessful rightest rebellion under Gen. Jose Sanjurjo occurred in August. This was too much like our native Hungary in 1918, so we obtained a booking in the Cirque d'Hiver in Paris for the months of January and February, 1933, and went back across the Pyrenees to France.

Seven years had come and gone since the day late in 1926 on which we said good-by to our friends in Paris and the Cirque d'Hiver and departed with Boyar, Romeo, Zebridge, and the bears for Barcelona. Now we were returning to Paris, not as bareback riders, but as La Troupe Asevera, a family foursome of high-school riders, with our horses Vulcan, Nobre, Luzero, Pinto Silgo, Immaculado, and Pinto, and an act that had already become known beyond the borders of Spain and Portugal. We were sans the bears, and Zebridge had succumbed to a tetanus infection in Portugal, but old Boyar and Romeo, pensioners now, in honorable retirement, were still very much with us. Inveterate troupers, both of them, they could not have adapted to any other kind of life.

In Paris and the Cirque d'Hiver again, among old friends and on a stellar program, along with Grock, the greatest of clowns,* we introduced our Asevera high-school act, "Fan-

---

* Grock, whose real name was Adrian Wettach, generally conceded to have been the greatest clown of modern times. The son of a Swiss clockmaker. Joined a travelling circus. Originally a rider, juggler, rope-dancer, acrobat and contortionist. One of highest paid figures in European show business. A master of grimace, with extraordinary vocal capabilities. A highly competent musician.

taisie Equestre Haute Ecole," to French audiences and French critics. Following are some of the Parisian press comments on these performances:

From *Les Hommes du Jour:* "As with the Empire around Damia, excellent numbers accompany Grock in the Winter Circus. Permit me to call your attention to the admirable high-school number of the four Aseveras, who are no other than the celebrated Konyots, Hungarian riders, two men, a woman and a lovely little girl of the age of 10, who already rides like a grownup horsewoman. Particularly worthy of note is a *soleil a cheval*, which made the galleries and loges stamp with enthusiasm."

From *L'Oeuvre:* "What joy in coming back to applaud the marvelous triple-high-school act of the Asevera family. With a marked Spanish rhythm, the horses danced, and, if I dare say so, in a clearly Iberian spirit. It is a truly astonishing thing, and all that the shoes of the horses lacked were *castanets*. These magnificent equestrians and an equestrienne in a white *mantilla* are to be highly praised, without forgetting the little girl who, on her piebald horse, seemed to have escaped from a Goya canvas."

X

As the Clouds Gathered

Inflation, Worker of Ruin

WITH OUR return to France and the Cirque d'Hiver in January, 1933, after six years in Spain and Portugal, we were entering upon a period that was to embrace the last years of our life in Europe. Thirteen years had passed since we left Budapest and went to Italy to begin a new life. We had worked hard and continuously for the rewards to be had from successful showmanship and had recouped our losses, only to have the value of our accumulation wiped out by inflation. The paying of debts and the practice of putting aside would have to begin all over again.

Actually, there had been an astonishing revival of the circus in Europe, with no lack of employment for those who had talent and good acts. We ourselves had been receiving our full share and had long since left adversity behind. We were even deluded, for a time, into thinking we were getting rich, until

101

inflation, that invisible worker of ruin, broke loose and pulled the mat of security right out from under us. However, it was still only 1933.

Hitler Comes to Power

Developments in Spain gave us reason to feel that it was well we had come to France, even though the state of French finances had become shaky. No comfort was to be found in what was transpiring in Germany, where the totalitarian regime of the Nazis was rapidly taking form. On Jan. 30, 1933, Hitler assumed the chancellorship, and in the months following the police power in Prussia came under the control of Goering. Goebbels became the minister of "public enlightenment" and propaganda, the trade unions were merged into the Labor Front, and the Constitution of Weimar was suspended.

Incident in a Friend's House

On March 4, 1933, we embarked on a tour of Germany and Poland with the Zirkus Jacob Busch, and toward the end of the engagement, while in Magdeburg on a weekend in the fall, elected to go to Berlin to visit an old friend. Adolph and Lilly, who were in Berlin at the time, were to be at our friend's house.

It was one of those golden days that mark the autumn in the north of Europe when we arrived at our destination and settled down to the renewal of an old acquaintance. Later on, in the afternoon, a sunburned boy of 12 or 13 in the swastika-marked khaki shirt and shorts of the Hitler Jugend entered the room. He was our host's son, and our host introduced him to us with fond paternal pride. Yes, he was a fine boy, his father said, and a good student, a member of the Hitler Jugend, too. Of course! The boy worked hard, too hard, he complained, adding, "They drill these young boys as though they were men and expect them to do their lessons in the evening, when they are dog-tired." The boy said nothing, and left the room, his father explaining that he had gone to the study to work on his assignments and that the poor boy would probably fall asleep.

Resuming our conversation, we exchanged what news we had of mutual friends and people we had known on the sawdust trail of the circus. What about that Austrian, an acrobat and bareback rider, who used to have an act with a German couple, *parforce* riders? He was the man who played the violin and was always falling in love, but had no wife. Whatever happened to him? And the Italian lady of the over-done dignity and violent temper, who made a good act on the *panneau* and thought she had a voice? Oh, yes, she was the woman who always wore pink in her act, and ran off with that fellow from somewhere in Russia, who had a Mongolian look about him. They went to Argentina.

And so it went, until finally and, I suppose, inevitably, the conversation turned to the subject of the Nazis. Well, we were in a friend's house, so Adolph and I, with the aid of some good pilsener, spoke freely, unguardedly. It would have been all right, or nothing would have come of it, had it not been for that young boy of the Hitler Jugend. If only he had been preoccupied with his lessons! Or better still, if only he had fallen asleep! Instead of that, he had been wide awake and listening in on our conversation, of which fact he abruptly informed us when, reappearing suddenly, he said:

"I heard what you said about my feuhrer. You are enemies and I am going to report you to my gauleiter." That is exactly what he did, as, one day, we were to learn. Because we had the status of Czecho-Slovak nationals, they could not touch us, so we were in no immediate danger. Later on it would be different.

Bertram Mills Catches Up with Us

Our 10 months on the road in Germany and Poland in the Zirkus Jacob Busch terminated in cold winter weather in Warsaw, where we remained for an additional month to ride *en haute ecole* in our act Fantasia Ecuestre Espanola in the Cyrk Staniewski. A booking with Gaston Dupréz, director of the Cirque d'Hiver, for a tenting tour of the French provinces necessitated our going back across Germany to France in the first week of March, 1934. Thereafter, for five months, we worked in the Cirque Medrano, the Goumont Palace, and on a program with the French comedian Fernandel in the Alhambra Music Hall in Paris. In Lille, in mid-September, 1934, Bernard Mills, one of the two sons of the late Capt. Bertram Mills, the great British circus owner and showman, came to see us.

Before leaving Portugal, we had had a letter from the senior Mills. He had had favorable comment on our Asevera high-school act, he wrote, and wanted to know where we were going to be working in the months ahead and on what dates. His inquiry was in accord with the practice he was known to follow, which was that of never hiring an act until either he or one of his sons, Cyril or Bernard, had seen it and approved of it. Bertram Mills was tireless in his search for talent and outstanding acts. With agents in many cities of the world, he and his sons covered thousands of miles annually. They particularly sought to find equestrian acts of first rate and special appeal, of which there were never too many. It was one of their agents who had told the Mills group about the Asevera family in Portugal. The agent had not learned that the name Asevera was a professional name and that the Aseveros were actually Konyots, so Bertram Mills did not know it either.

The Annual Christmas Show

Bernard was sent to Madrid to see our act there. He was delayed enroute, however, and missed us. We had gone on tour, so he started in pursuit, but failed to catch up with us because of detours made necessary by the political and civil strife. Bernard went to Paris later on, and saw our act, but the terms he had been authorized to offer us did not meet with our approval. He returned, months later, this time to Lille, going there by plane, with adequately generous terms. It was in a portable wooden building of the Cirque Poutier that he signed us up after lunch for the Annual Christmas Show of the Bertram Mills Circus at Olympia, in London. After two months in Belgium with the Cirque de Jonghe in Liege and the Cirque Royale in Brussels, we crossed the channel with Vulcan, Nobre, Pinto Silgo, Luzero, Immaculado, and Pinto, and, of course, Boyar and Romeo, and went by train to London, arriving there in time for the Grand Opening of the Bertram Mills Circus on Dec. 28, 1934, in the great striped tent under the dome of Olympia.

The Grand Opening at Olympia was the expression and the achievement of a master showman and organizer. The late Bertram Mills had a flair for the spectacular without affront to art. He knew the business of entertainment, and understood the niceties of arrangement and ceremony that give elegance and distinction to the setting, enhancing the impact of great performance and a gala occasion. At Olympia, the circus was not only circus at its best, but it took on the flavor of an important social event, and was, indeed, a highlight of London's Christmas season. The opening performance was preceded by a luncheon for 1,200 guests, among whom were a congregation of peers and peeresses of the realm, the lord mayor and the mayors of the boroughs, cabinet ministers, members of Parliament and a cross-section of the prominent in the business, professional, and social life of London. Princess Alice was the guest of honor and the Earl of Lonsdale, President of the Bertram Mills Olympia Circus, proposed the toast. The show opened to a fanfare by the trumpeters of the Royal Horse Guards, and a military band led the grand parade. Lord Lonsdale presented flowers to the women performers. The Duke of York, later King George VI, and his wife, Elizabeth, came to one of the later performances with their two little daughters, the Princesses Elizabeth and Margaret Rose, and we had the honor of being presented to them at a reception presided over by Lord Lonsdale.

The calibre of the acts in the Bertram Mills Circus of 1934-35 (Dec. 28, 1934, through Jan. 16, 1935) was in conformity with the panoply at Olympia. Alberti, wizard of the perch-pole, made his sensational swinging mast act. The Flying Concellos, Marie Antoinette and Arthur, with Everard White as the catcher, made their act on the flying trapeze. Rudolph Matthies was there with his Hagenbeck tigers, Franz Althoff with his elephants; and Kling with his bicycle-riding, umbrella-carrying chimpanzees. Tamara (the Flying Swallow), C. J. Blumenfeld, and Somba Hamida provided competition for the Concellos on the trapeze with a combined aerial act: The Four Bronetts, Bruno, Kalle, Sven, and Tini, celebrated entree clowns, presented their famous water-spilling act, and spilled enough water to drown a company. There were the Five Slatnachs, trick cyclists; the Lai Foun Chinese troupe of contortionists, acrobats, and jugglers, and the Three Raspinis, lady balancers. Czeslaw Mroczkowski presented the Bertram Mills liberty horses, grays, creams, and 16 Lipizzaners. Milly Yelding did a trick riding act, in which she worked nine stallions while astride three, and the Loyal Repensky troupe of 13 bareback riders performed with six horses.

As for our own act, it was described by the critics as follows:

From the *London Sunday Times:* ". . . the grace and loveliness of Los Aseverōs' *haute école* performance from Portugal will live long in memory."

From *Horse and Hounds:* "Los Aseveros, a Portuguese family, provide one of the finest and most graceful of *haute ecole* exhibitions. There is a style and polish about this act, which should commend itself to the many riding enthusiasts who might wish to learn something about balance and the center of gravity."

William G. Bosworth, in his book *Wagon Wheels,* wrote:

"Turning from liberty horses to high-school riding, there are many who think the Asevera family put on the most elegant equestrian act to visit England. The quartet consists of father, mother, daughter and son, and they appear in the ring in the romantic national dress of Portugal. Their grave dignity and grace is enhanced by the costumes of the ladies, who, in white, with *mantilla,* sweeping frilled skirts and high combs, riding white horses, are redolent of the essence of equestrianism.

"Thousands rose to the brilliant riding of the Los Aseveros family, father, mother, son and daughter, in the national dress of Portugal."

Back to the Continent

Engagements to work on the stage in the variety theatres took us back to the continent and kept us busy for the rest of the winter. In the Spring we went on a tenting tour of Poland with the Cyrk Staniewski and finished the season in Warsaw. Late in the Fall we were on stage again—in the Karlsbader Orpheum, in Karlsbad, during Christmas week; in the Margaretner Orpheum and the Ronacher Varieté, Vienna, thereafter. It was while we were in Vienna that the Schumann brothers, Oscar, Ernst, and Willie, senior members of that leading family, booked us by mail for April and May with their circus in Copenhagen. They had not seen our Asevera high-school act but were sufficiently impressed by what they had heard about it to offer us a contract we were likely to accept. They commissioned me at the same time to buy them six gray Arabians, two Lipizzaners, and a pair of matched blacks for their liberty acts. I procured the Arabians in Yugoslavia, in former Hungarian territory; the blacks and the two Lipizzaners in Austria, and two more of the latter breed, Pluto and Favorite, for our own string. The agreement with the Schumanns was that I begin training their Lipizzaners at once, which I did, turning them over later on in Copenhagen to young Albert and Max, after acquainting the young trainers with the procedure I had been following.

It was at this time, as I recall it, while we were in the Cirkus Schumann in Copenhagen, that we met Tom Mix, the American cowboy star of moving picture fame. He was working in the Cirkus Belli with a troupe of trick ropers and cowboy riders. He had his famous horse Tony with him, of course.

In Copenhagen I bought six boxer dogs and began training

them for a basketball act. In this act, two men held the baskets, which were attached to poles, a balloon serving as the basketball. The dogs were taught to nudge the balloon into the basket with their noses, and they were divided into two teams. One of the teams always represented the community in which we were playing, and the men who held the baskets knew how to build up the score of the home team without making it apparent that they were doing so. I offered this act during my last years in Europe and for two seasons in the Ringling Brothers and Barnum & Bailey Circus in the United States in 1940.

In the Tower Circus at Blackpool, England

The Asevera family, whose high-school act is the best I have ever seen beamed with pleasure when Mr. Lockhart tendered congratulations.

—W. G. Bosworth in the 1936 Autumn issue of *The Sawdust Ring*, official publication of the Circus Fans Association of Great Britain, with reference to the Tower Circus, Blackpool, England, season of 1936.

The first of June, 1936, found us in England and about to begin a long engagement in the Tower Circus in Blackpool. Unlike the countries of continental Europe, England does not have permanent circuses. But the circus at Blackpool, with a season extending from June 1 to the end of October, is the nearest thing to it. One of the great circuses of the world, it is known for its elaborate water pantomimes and the hydraulic floor, which can be lowered six feet for flooding, thus making it possible to convert the ring into a lake.

George Lockhart, whose father was a noted elephant trainer, was the equestrian director at Blackpool and was a leading personage in the Tower Circus for many years. Another leader of those years was William McAllister, better known as "Doodles," one of England's favorite clowns. A stellar performance in 1936 was that of the Berosini family on the high wire. Josephine Berosini, then a girl of 16, has since reached the pinnacle of high wire performance in her own right and is now the wife of my son Alexander.

Pluto and Favorite, the Lipizzaners we had acquired in Austria, were now in our string and in process of training. That there was a new interest in horses of this breed was evidenced by the number of people who stopped at our stalls to look at them and ask questions. Prior to World War I, horses of the Lipizzaner breed were rarely seen off their exclusive preserves in Austria-Hungary. And performances by the Lipizzaners of the Spanische Hofreitschule (the Spanish Riding School) were for privileged eyes, to be seen inside the school, a proud patronage of the House of Hapsburg, within the walls of the Hofburg.

After the war of 1914-1918 the school had to send its horses and riders out into the world to earn the wherewithal for survival, and the English had their first chance to acclaim them in 1927 at Olympia. Lipizzaners began finding their way into private hands and into the circus in the decade of the 1920's. Felix Salten's novel *Florian* and a moving picture version of it dramatized the wonderful white horses of Vienna as never before and aroused an entirely new admiration for them.

One day, while evincing much interest in our two Lipizzaners and admiring the beauty and musculature of Immaculado, the Spanish Andalusian Luzero and our Portuguese grays, as they stood in the clean straw in their stalls at Blackpool, a newspaper writer, interviewing the *artistes* in the circus, expressed surprise at the presence of our old bareback horses Boyar and Romeo in the group.

"Surely, these big horses don't belong to you," he said. "They look like draft horses."

"Yes," I replied. "They are our old bareback horses. We've had them a long time."

"But, Mr. Asevera, I thought you said you gave up bareback riding in 1929."

"That is right," I said, "Boyar and Romeo have been good horses. They're pensioners now and we always have them with us." This struck the man as being extraordinary.

"Do you mean to say," he interjected, "that you have been feeding those big horses all that time and hauling them around with you on your travels? Why, I think that is remarkable." I did not reply. Boyar and Romeo nickered and I gave them each a lump of sugar.

Both these old horses were unusually intelligent within their scheme of things, Boyar especially. Frequently, on arriving at a new destination, we rode our high-school horses from the railroad station to the circus or music hall and Boyar and Romeo carried out the rear on their own. Our horses were fast, flat-footed walkers, and Boyar, who was older than Romeo, often found the going too brisk. On such occasions, coming up from behind at a gallop and going on ahead, he would stop in front of us and make a barrier of himself by standing broadside across our path. This was in protest against the too-rapid gait, and it brought us to a halt. After getting what he wanted, which was a slowdown and a brief rest at the stand, Boyar would move to the side, and, as we went on again at a slower pace, would resume his position with Romeo at the rear of the column.

There were times when it was necessary to transport the horses across town by truck. On such occasions Boyar, unhaltered and entirely free, would not enter the truck until the rest of the horses had been loaded, and he was just as intent on being the first horse out of the truck. His career as a bareback horse was over, to be sure, but that was not to prevent him from becoming a traffic policeman. Invariably after backing out of the truck, he assumed a position on the street that was obviously calculated to block off such traffic as there was, and he held it until the last of the horses had been unloaded. That he enjoyed his self-assumed role was made clear by the frolicsome way in which he came up to us at that juncture to receive an apple, a pear, a carrot, or a lump of sugar for a job well done.

Our act in the Tower Circus, "Los Aseveros, the Aristocrats of High-School Riders," was the same as at Olympia. From Blackpool we went back to the continent and concluded the year 1936 with return engagements on the stage in Vienna and

Prague, in which we rode Favorite and Pluto for the first time in our Asevera high-school act. We had a contract to fill in Riga, Latvia, for the month of January and the first half of February, 1937. European skies were clouding over. It was very cold in Latvia, but the attitude of the people was warm. We found Riga a clean, bright city, where nearly everyone could speak Russian and nobody wanted to. While there, I bought Kaitan, a bay Latvian trotter of Russian Orloff breeding. Kaitan would have met a hard fate if he had been in Latvia three years later, so he was a lucky horse when I bought him and took him away.

One cold morning in Warsaw, on our way back from Riga, Boyar was down in his stall. When we found he could not get up, I called the veterinarian. The old horse was suffering from paralysis of the kidneys and could not survive. At the age of 36, he had come to the end of the road. So, with heavy hearts, we said good-bye to him and had the veterinarian put him painlessly to sleep. Without Boyar next to him, Romeo lost interest in life and a few months later died in his sleep. His heart just stopped beating.

XI

The Swastika Spreads Its Arms

Captain X

WHILE in Copenhagen, in the Cirkus Belli in late 1937, we decided to go to Czecho-Slovakia to organize a circus of our own there. Since the ruinous inflation of 1923, which wiped out our German, Austrian, and Hungarian holdings, we had been depositing our earnings in Czecho-Slovakia. Despite our Hungarian nationality, the war had converted us into citizens of Czecho-Slovakia, and we had come to think of that new state as a haven of stability and prosperity. So, with the termination of the Cirkus Belli contract, after sending our grooms, horses, boxer dogs, and equipment ahead by train, we left Copenhagen in our automobile, bound for Prague.

Our troubles began at the German border, where we were subjected to a rude and exhaustive questioning and a personal going-over that was exasperating. Our trunks and luggage were

113

turned upside down and emptied of their contents, and in their inspection of our automobile the German border officials saw fit to take the tires off the rims of the wheels, all four of them, and to rip up and remove the floor mats, front and back. The timing of our departure from Copenhagen was unfortunate because it coincided with Mussolini's visit to Nazi Germany and his tour of the country in the company of Hitler. All foreign automobiles were being held up for a long wait before clearance, and when cleared were required to take on two detectives, who accompanied them for the first 100 miles or so into German territory. We were allowed to go on from the border only on the condition that we would report at Gestapo headquarters in every town, village, and hamlet we came to. The day-long delay at the border was enough of an ordeal itself, but the rough treatment meted out there was repeated at succeeding stops.

In one place, the commandant at Gestapo headquarters, not satisfied with seeing me only, demanded to see the members of my family. When I explained that my wife was too ill to leave the automobile, which was a fact, he showed signs of rage, and barked out:

"Have I not already told you that I want your wife to come here and report? If she is too sick to walk, you will have to carry her in. Go and get her."

At the next town, I had to gird myself at the prospect of going through all that again, but there was nothing else to do. So, at a somber-looking gray stone building, which was dark and cold, like a mortuary, I went up to a guard and was escorted once more to the office of the commandant. The thoughts that coursed through my head as I followed the long-coated, helmeted, booted six-footer, who was the guard, were as dark as the long corridor, but to turn back was out of the question. A heavy oaken door now opened. I walked in and found myself facing another of Himmler's captains, the commandant, who, looking at me with a stony face, told the guard to leave, got up from his chair and closed the door, returned and sat down. Thereupon his expression changed. Incomprehensible though it seemed, I was now looking into a friendly face, and the face was one I knew I had seen somewhere before. The captain spoke.

"Arthur Konyot," he said in a lowered voice. "Do you recognize me?"

He then pronounced his name and asked me if I did not now remember him. I replied that he looked familiar and I was aware of having known someone with that name, but I still could not place him.

"We were young together," he continued. "You and your brothers and I used to get together in Budapest, Mahrisch-Ostrau, and Vienna. Don't you remember?"

Now I remembered. I had known him in the circus. The captain (I shall call him Captain X) smiled, and it was a warm smile. We shook hands, and in the voice of one fearing we might be overheard, my friend of better days, a captain now of the Nazi Gestapo but a friend indeed, leaned forward across the desk and said:

"I am sorry, old friend, but, as I am sure you can understand, I have my duty to perform. However, nothing is going to happen to you or your family, if you do exactly as I say. Listen to me carefully. You and your brother Adolph are on the blacklist. Did you know that? You suspected it, you say. All right. Now, here are my instructions. Continue to stop at Gestapo headquarters at each town you come to and give them your name. I will take care of the rest. Tell no one of this conversation. Remember what I have said. *Gruss Gott. Auf wiedersehen.*"

I never heard anything from or about Captain X again. For the rest of our trip across Germany I followed his instructions, and on reporting to the Gestapo we were released promptly in every instance, with no further ado.

I have saved a 1937 clipping from the *Nationaltidande*, a Copenhagen daily, which says of the Cirkus Belli: "First of all is the Spanish equestrian family, the Aseveras, whom one remembers from the Cirkus Schumann last year. There are two women in white crinoline dresses and two men in torero costumes, who all four sit to perfection in their saddles, and without use of whip or spur ride their pure Andalusian horses over the sawdust in the ring in step with the music from Carmen. The horses are in genuine and ornately embellished Spanish bridles and breast-plates, and the act makes a magnificent picture."

Walled In

In Gerkau (Jirkov), in the Sudetenland, Czecho-Slovakia, in 1938, I put a lot of money into animals and equipment and started a circus. The Sudetenland comprised the German-speaking districts of Northern Bohemia, and the propaganda for independence from Prague and even for absorption into Hitler's Reich was in full swing. Czechs had become *persona non grata,* and as Czech nationals we soon found ourselves considerably less than welcome. So purposeful and well organized was the hostility that our circus was boycotted and we ourselves all but ostracized. Under such compulsion, we moved on to the south of the German-conscious Sudetenland, hoping for a better reception, but encountered more hostility—the hostility of the Czechs toward the Magyars. The fact that we were citizens made no difference. The region from whence we came was still former Hungarian territory, although it had been a part of Czecho-Slovakia for nearly 20 years. In the eyes of the Czechs we were still Hungarians or Magyars.

As we moved out of one town into another, with the boycott continuing, and had to defray the cost of feed, transportation, wages, lighting, fees to the municipalities, etc., our money in hand was going fast, with far less coming in than was being paid out. Soon we had to go into debt to keep going, and when we were unable to meet the demands of the creditors, our property was seized. This went on until we had been divested of practically everything but our six high-school horses, the boxer dogs we brought from Denmark, and our tents. Even these would have been taken if it had not been for the law which protected the debtor in the possession of property he could prove to be indispensable to him in making a living. Adolph and Lilly had joined forces with us on our coming to Czecho-Slovakia, but with the substance of our circus going for debt and the losses mounting, there was no point in their remaining with us. They departed, accordingly, and once again went their separate way. The way Adolph and Lilly chose was to remain in Czecho-Slovakia.

After losing my automobile, I used to rent a bicycle on which to pedal my way to the next town or village to get permission to conduct a show there. Our tents were taken by creditors, so that all we had left for shelter was a piece of canvas, which we tied to trees to sleep under and transported from one place to another with a rented horse and wagon. We were now giving our show in the open air and living from hand to mouth. I offered a liberty act with Nobre and Pinto Silgo and a basketball act with the boxers. Alex made a trick riding act, and he and Dorita danced. Then we rode together, all four of us, just as we had done in the Cirque d'Hiver, the Bertram Mills Circus at Olympia, the Cirkus Schumann in Copenhagen, and the leading variety theatres and music halls in Paris, Prague, and Vienna.

In one village we were at a loss for a place to keep our horses and might not have found any but for the good Samaritanism of a friendly priest, who stopped, in passing by, and began to converse. He spoke German and French, so we were able to tell him of our plight.

"I have a place for your horses and dogs," he said, "on the parish grounds, and I take pleasure in inviting you all to be my guests in the parish house." He brought us food and drink, spoke kind words, and gave us his blessings, saying, further, as he took leave, that he would pray for us.

At another village, a man of distinguished appearance remained after our performance to thank us for what he had seen. Our horsemanship was regal, he said, and the whole performance had delighted him. It reminded him of the Hofreitschule in Vienna, and he had not seen better. This led to an extended conversation, which was in French, and, before leaving, our

kind and appreciative visitor said he would return on the morrow, and he did, bringing with him a wagonload of grain and
hay for the horses, the choicest of food and meats for us, and
wine from his own vineyards.

Our situation now began to improve as we journeyed from
village to village, and through our best efforts, after which we
passed the hat, acquired a little money, enough to buy feed for
the horses and the dogs, to keep body and soul together, and
even to buy more canvas. The Czechs continued to look askance
at Magyars; the organized hostility and the boycott continued.
But enough people were attracted to our show to enable us to
make a ring, which we roped off against free-loaders, and to
rent chairs for the spectators. Moving eastward into Slovakia—
in flight actually—we came at length to Zilina, not far from
Rajec, where my father was born, in former Hungarian territory and only a few miles from the Polish frontier. We had rela-
tives and friends there and in nearby places who might prove
helpful. It was after the Munich agreement, however. Austria
was under Hitler, and Czecho-Slovakia was falling apart.
Czechs and Magyars were becoming less and less welcome by
the day. If we could not stay here, where were we to go? One
thing was certain: we could not go back. Since we were on the
blacklist of the conquering Nazi, we had reached the point of
no return.

On Oct. 8, 1938, Slovakia was pronounced an autonomous
state under the "protection" of Hitler's Germany, and with that
the anti-Hungarian, anti-Czech agitation came to a head. A
proclamation was issued from Bratislava ordering all Czechs
and Magyars to leave the country within 24 hours. That nulli-
fied our privilege to conduct a show in Zilina and left us with no
alternative but to leave Slovakia, our former Hungarian homeland, at once. Where to go? Walled in as we were on three sides,
there was only one direction possible, and that was forward in
the direction of Poland. However, on Oct. 8 the Polish border
was closed, and that raised a fourth wall to block our escape.

In Zilina I had an old friend, a former high official in the

Czecho-Slovak ministry, and it was just possible that he might know of a way to get us across the border into Poland. If he didn't, we were doomed. There was little time. Hoping desperately, I went to see him and obtained a new lease on life when he said he would be able to procure a baggage car for our use and that it would be at the railroad station waiting for us.

"Go to the station," he said, "with your horses and dogs and everything you have. By the time you get there the car will be there. Put the horses and dogs, your luggage, and equipment into the car. Get into it yourselves and stay in it. I can say no more. We are working against time. God speed."

With our very lives in the balance, we outdid ourselves in getting to the station. The car was there, and we proceeded to load everything and to get into the car ourselves. An hour of fear and anxiety passed, relieved finally when a small engine backed up to our car, hooked on to it, pulled it beyond the station to a main track, and left it there. Soon another locomotive, a bigger one with two sealed baggage cars in tow, appeared out of nowhere, and before we knew it we were moving away from Zilina, with the cowcatcher on the locomotive pointed in the direction of the Polish border, some 20 miles away.

I don't seem to remember much of anything about the journey to the border. Perhaps that is because I was projecting my mind. My memories become clear again at the point where we came to a stop. It was dark by then, very dark. Manya had just commented on the fact, when we saw a light moving to and fro at the side of the car just ahead. The brakeman was signaling the locomotive that he had uncoupled our car. Thereupon the locomotive and its two sealed baggage cars pulled away from us, turned onto a switch track and disappeared, only to reappear shortly thereafter, going in the opposite direction on a parallel track back to Zilina.

Where were we in our lone baggage car out there on that track in the stillness of the night? In Poland? Or were we still in Slovakia? A railroad man now appeared with his lamp and addressed us in Slovakian. Alas! We were still in Slovakia. I spoke to him in German, and he understood. Speaking in a Slavonic German, he wanted to know who we were, from whence we had come, by whose authority we had procured the car and where we thought we were going in it. I offered him an explanation, and our hearts sank when he replied:

"I am not questioning your right to be here in this car, but I tell you again that the border has been closed and you will not be allowed to cross."

I asked him how far we were from the border.

"You are on it," he said. "It is only a stone's throw ahead."

Suddenly, almost before the man had finished speaking, a locomotive came up the track from behind and, with scarcely a jolt, pushed us across the border into Poland. With that accomplished, it backed away and left our car to resume its lone stand on the track, this time in Polish territory.

So we were in Poland. But what now? There were no lights in the car, and we had no flashlight, only candles. The hours passed, two hours, three hours, four, five, and six. I had got out of the car, and as I stood there on the tracks peering into the night and searching my brain for a step to take, I saw a dim light far ahead. Something within impelled me to go to the source of it. So up the tracks I walked for what seemed a very long distance, the light growing brighter as I continued walking, until at last it was revealed to have been not just a single light but the many lights of the first Polish railroad station beyond the border. I went into the station and sought out the station master, who, to my relief, spoke German, and could understand me when I told him about our baggage car back there in the darkness and of how desperate we were to find refuge in Poland, and why.

"All right, my good man," he said. "You stay here while I send an engine after your car." Within minutes, I heard a high, screaming whistle and the sound of escaping steam as a locomotive came to life on a siding, backed up on to the main tracks and, with its bell clanging, began to chug its way in the direction from whence I had come. Time itself seemed now to have become invigorated, because it was only a matter of minutes before that wonderful little Polish locomotive, the headlights on its tender growing brighter on the tracks, came back to the station with our baggage car in tow.

Manya and Dorita got out of the car and went into the cafe in the station, where, after watering the horses and taking the dogs out for an airing, my son and I joined them. We were all hungry but too tired to know it. Nevertheless, we ordered a meal, and when the time came to pay and I put my Czecho-Slovak money down on the counter, the proprietor of the cafe would not accept it. Manya then took her diamond ring off her finger, handed it to the man, and told him to keep it until we could send him the money. At just about that moment the station master reappeared, accompanied by a customs officer. The latter asked for our visas and the admission papers for the horses and dogs. When I told him I had none, he shrugged his shoulders in a gesture of futility and said that in such case we could not remain in Poland longer than 24 hours and that he would have to push our car back across the border into Slovakia at the end of that time.

I had the sensation of being imprisoned within four opposing walls, very high, black walls, and they were closing in. This much I knew: either we would find refuge in Poland or we had come to the end. I had a gun. It was loaded, and I thought about that. I looked at my wife and little daughter. They had been weeping quietly. Now they were praying. Had not the kindly priest said he would pray for us? Perhaps he was praying for us now. I could pray. So could my son. And we did. A remarkable thing now happened. It was like a deliverance. An idea came forward from the agony of my thoughts and with impelling clarity presented itself. It was the solution. Why, of course, I would go into the station and telephone Bronislaw Staniewski, proprietor of the Cyrk Staniewski in Warsaw. He was a friend of mine and an able one. For this I had only Czecho-Slovak money, so I would have to prevail upon the good will of the station master to let me use his private telephone, with the promise to reimburse him at the earliest possible moment.

"Use it," he said, "I trust you and want to help you."

Fortune came over to our side for the moment, at least, when I heard the familiar voice of Staniewski coming clear.

"Hello, Arthur. Go on. I hear you."

I do not remember my own words, but I do remember what Staniewski said in reply:

"I will go at once to the ministerium on your behalf. Stay there in the cafe and wait for my instructions. Don't worry. I will get you in." The relief that came to us with these words was so great that all four of us, sitting there in the cafe and waiting, dozed off into intermittent slumber. The clock struck 12. Waiting. Now it was half past 12, then 1 o'clock. Still waiting. I heard the clock strike 2, and a few minutes afterward was wide awake when the station master came into the cafe and in a loud voice called out:

"Hello, I have good news for you, Konyot. You have permission to remain in Poland for such time as you may require to procure visas for entrance into some other country. The customs officers have been instructed by a higher authority to let you and your family pass, the horses and dogs included."

He had received a personal telegram from Staniewski, and he read it: "Send the Konyots and their horses and dogs on the first train to Warsaw. Buy tickets for them at my expense." We were met in Warsaw by Saniewski, and trucks from the circus were at the station to transport our horses to the stables. At our hotel, we went to bed and slept the sleep of exhaustion.

The Cyrk Staniewski had a full program, so we were not needed. Nevertheless, Staniewski took us on. He couldn't pay us what we could ordinarily command, but what he did pay enabled us to remunerate him for the cost of our transportation from the Slovak border to Warsaw. In the meantime, we accepted the offer of a contract from the Cirk Salamonsky in Riga, for June and July, 1939, but were unable to get Latvian visas and transport permits across Lithuania. I therefore telephoned

Tabacnik, director of the circus, who said he would intervene in the matter. Shortly I had a letter from him saying that our train had a right of passage across Lithuania, though we could not get off in that country. Our Latvian visas would be at the border, he said. They were not, so I telephoned Tabacnik again.

"Stay where you are," he said. "If there has been any delay, I will hurry it up."

The baggage car containing our horses and dogs had been uncoupled and was now on a siding. The train, of course, had gone on. There was a neutral zone, a narrow strip of land between the two countries, and we went into a restaurant there. A long uncomfortable day passed, and half of another day. A railroad official then came in, paging Konyot.

"Go over to the Latvian customs depot," he said. "Your visas are there. Here, take these."

He then handed me a certificate, signifying that our fare had been paid, along with four accommodations to Riga on the next train. We left that night and arrived in Riga the next day. Tabacnik was at the station to meet us. He found the baggage car with our horses and dogs in it, but there was no sign of us. No wonder! We were fast asleep, all four of us, on the hard wooden benches of the coach, and were not discovered until a train crewman came upon us a few minutes later and awakened us with the announcement, "Wake up! You're in Riga."

The Cirk Salamonsky had a full and strong program, which included the equestrian acts, with 60 horses, of the Zirkus Strassburger. In other words, Tabacnik did not need us in Riga any more than Staniewski needed us in Poland. Nevertheless, on hearing that we were in Warsaw and that it was our plan to come to Riga, he had offered us a contrast and made a place for us. So we rode again in Latvia as the Aseveras in our Fantasia Ecuestre Espanola. In Warsaw, Bronislaw Staniewski had generously advanced funds to us, and I now had the problem of paying him back. Money I did not have; horses I did have. I did not want to leave Riga without sending Staniewski what I owed him, and the only way I could raise the money was by selling one of my well-trained horses. Hans Strassburger, proprietor of the Zirkus Strassburger and an able equestrian, wanted to buy Favorite, one of the two Lipizzaners I acquired in Austria in 1935, so I sold the horse to him, and from the proceeds paid off my debt to Staniewski. From Strassburger, I acquired for a low price the gray Portuguese horse Dynamite, a former "bull" horse of the *tourado*. Dynamite was lame when I bought him, but after three years of rest, care, and treatment, he became sound again.

When Hitler marched into Prague on March 15, 1939, our investments and savings in Czecho-Slovakia were lost to us forever. If I had learned then, or during the ensuing weeks, what I did not learn until four or five years later, I would have known that I was never going to see my brother Adolph again. He was caught in the trap of events, and died, no doubt, at the hands of the invaders. If only he and Lilly had come with us on our flight through Slovakia to Poland! Lilly survived, but she does not like to talk about those days. With regard to Staniewski and Tabacnik, I regret to say that both of those fine Polish gentlemen were killed in the war that devastated their country from the east and west only a few months after we saw them for the last time.

XII

Rainbow in the West

Escape

IN RIGA I signed up by mail for engagements in Copenhagen, with the Cirkus Jean Houck, and in Paris, with Jerome Medrano. In the meantime, the prospects for "peace in our time," as of the pact of Munich, had been shattered and the storm clouds of war were gathering in the west. The states of Central Europe that were not already under the domination of Hitler's Germany were in no position to resist coercion, and a showdown seemed near.

All overland routes to the west were out of the question for us, so our avenue of escape would have to be by water. We could go to Copenhagen by way of the Gulf of Riga and the Baltic, we thought, but when we found that all passenger vessels going there touched at German ports, the fact was brought home to us that our troubles were not over yet.

After extensive and fruitless inquiries, we asked at a last
Danish shipping office if they did not have some kind of ship
going to Copenhagen that did not touch at a German port. The
response was that they did have. It was a cargo steamer, and it
was due in Riga in time to sail from there for Copenhagen the
following week. But it did not carry passengers. That we were
desperate was made evident by Manya's tearful entreaties, and
the shipping officer said:

"There is nothing we can do for you at this office, but I sug-
gest that you go to see the captain when the ship docks here in
a few days. The captain is the master of his ship, after all, and
if he chooses to grant an exception in your case in order to take
you and your family to Copenhagen, there is no rule that can
prevent him from doing so. If you would like me to, I will be
glad to give you a letter of introduction. Call us in the early
week and we will then be able to tell you when the ship is due
and the dock it will tie up at."

When, in due course, the ship did come in, we hurried to the
dock with our letter. The captain, though at first indisposed,
listened sympathetically to Manya's pleas, and, moved by her
tears, said:

"All right, Mrs. Konyot and Mr. Konyot. You can come with
us. I only have one cabin with a bed in it. It is small, Mrs. Konyot, but you and your daughter may have it. Mr. Konyot, you
and your boy will have to find your own bunks. I can provide
you with blankets."

Our impatience to be under way was great, and we were at
the dock with our horses and dogs at an early hour on the day of
sailing. The voyage took three days. We had our meals at the
captain's big table, where the fare was good, and we found the
crew a fine and jolly group of seafaring men. My son and I slept
comfortably on beds of hay and straw alongside the horses.

When I went to the French consulate in Copenhagen to procure our French visas, I asked the consul if there was going to
be a war. He didn't think so. It was a relieving thought, if not
exactly a convincing one, with which we were able to sidetrack

our concern as we left Copenhagen by sea for Antwerp on the way to Paris. Arriving in Antwerp, we stopped there overnight, and on the next morning took the train for Paris, leaving Alex behind to clear the horses and to come on as soon as he could. At the Cirque Medrano the following day, a telegram came from Alex saying that the French border had been closed and that the car was being held up there. Jerome Medrano, who was both resourceful and influential, immediately got busy, and through his intercession the car was allowed to pass and continue on to Paris. The next day, the second World War began.

Paris, 1939: War Comes

When war came, the circus closed, but it opened again in two weeks, playing only three times a week, with the windows painted black on the outside. Enemy reconnaissance planes were reported over Paris at frequent intervals, night and day, and the air-raid sirens screamed out their warnings at each report. The night warnings sent people into their basements. The day warnings sent them into the subways. At our hotel the guests joined in to dig a trench shelter eight feet in depth, covering it with planks and earth. Instead of affording protection to the occupants, it would probably have been their tomb had a bomb dropped near it.

Despite the air raids, or the fear of them, and the disruptions and interruptions of wartime, the Parisians came in increasing numbers to the Cirque Medrano, in which we worked continuously until John Ringling North came to Paris and contracted us for a two-year engagement in the Ringling Brothers and Barnum & Bailey Circus. That was in November.

In December the French government issued a ruling which required all physically fit male foreigners of military age to join a newly created legion of non-citizens. Thereupon, my son Alexander, then 25, enlisted. Through the good offices and efforts of influential friends, however, we succeeded in obtaining a leave of absence for six months and an American visa for him. Six weeks later, Manya, Dorita, and Alex sailed from Marseilles on the S. S. *Excalibur* of the American Export Line for New York with Vulcan, Pluto, and Kaitan, the Shetland pony Sultan and the boxer dogs, arriving in time for the opening of the season of 1930 in Madison Square Garden.

Two weeks later I followed them on the S. S. *Exeter,* of the same line, with Nobre, Luzero, and Dynamite. On board the *Exeter,* with the horses safely in their stalls, I cabled my family that I was about to sail, and an hour thereafter, at sea, had a cablegram from Manya in New York saying that they had arrived and all was well. After that, feeling more relaxed than in years, I retired to my cabin and took a nap. When I awakened it was past the noon hour of the next day.

In my crowded life, the last 26 years of which had been lived against a background of war, revolution, and the troubles that follow in train, there had been no time for reflection on all that had gone by. But those days at sea on the *Exeter* made way for such thoughts. At 52, and no worse for the wear despite some long, hard years, I was intent on the future, on our new life in America, soon to begin, on unfinished business. Was this a dream coming true? It did seem so, because I had always wanted to go back to the United States. It was in the year 1912, 28 years before, that we sailed from New York, my parents, brothers, and sisters, et al., on our homeward-bound journey, after three memorable years with the Barnum & Bailey Circus. The effects of that experience had never quite worn off. My thoughts went back to that day, to my last view of the Statue of Liberty, the tall buildings on Manhattan fading from sight, and my resolve then and there, that some day, I would return.

The late John Ringling made almost yearly trips to Europe over the intervening years, and he rarely failed to look me up. Time and again he urged me to return to the United States:

"Konyot," he would ask, "when are you coming back? Why not this year? You know what I have always told you: A contract is yours for the asking."

Why, then, did I not come? Why had I not accepted a single

one of John Ringling's repeated offers? The answer is that in Europe contracts are made well ahead and that I was always booked up too far in advance. I could not break the contracts I had accepted, not even to go to America.

One does not discard the past just by getting on a ship and sailing away from the scene of it to a new clime. My life in old Europe had been of too many years' duration, too rich in associations and experience, and too full of happiness and solid achievement, as well as of trial and trouble, not to have left the stored-up effects of its impact. So it was that during those restful days on shipboard while en route to America, a medley of thoughts, memories, and impressions from the past came crowding in upon me. The soothing sleep-inducing salt air probably had something to do with it, because I found myself wandering off repeatedly into a half-sleep. It was then that the past, disconnected but vividly returning bits of it, recovered momentarily from over the many long years, came back into focus. Oh, yes, there were a few times when I awakened with a start and in a cold sweat, to be relieved at having wakened. Those were memories, too, and not nightmares, but there were not many, and recurrences were few. Ahead lay America, not far away now. There was a rainbow in the West.

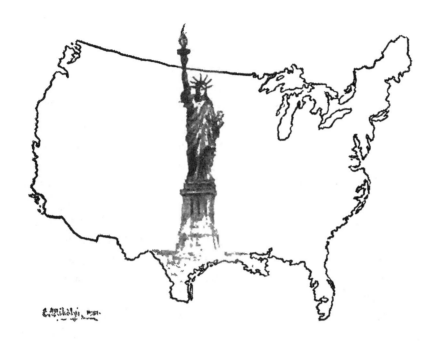

XIII

A Dream Comes True

Five Years with Ringling Brothers and Barnum & Bailey

ARRIVING IN NEW YORK, I was met by Herbert Duvall, an agent for the circus, who had come to facilitate my getting through the customs. A truck was at the dock to take my horses to Madison Square Garden, and I went directly there myself. My family were awaiting me. The next day, Dorita underwent surgery and was unable to work for three months.

A week at Boston Garden, Boston, Mass., came next, and from there the circus took off on its annual seven and one-half month tour of this broad, wonderful land. The country had changed since 1911, of course, and chiefly in the number and magnitude of things. Gone were the horses from the cities and towns, and to a great extent, even, from the farms. There were changes in the circus, too: more especially in the method of transport and

131

operation. Thirty years before, in the Barnum & Bailey Circus
I remembered so well, 300 baggage horses had done the work
of transport from train to lot, and elephants were used in the
heaviest work, pulling the tent ropes, and so on. In 1940, you
had to look for the horse tent; elephants were still used on
occasions, but not often. Animal power had been superseded
almost entirely by truck, tractor, Caterpillar, and automobile.
Progress! With a picture in my mind's eye of row on row of the
great, strapping draft horses in the circus of yesterday, I remembered the pride the circuses used to take in their wealth of
baggage stock and reflected on the fact that it was the kind of
pride you can't transfer to machinery. The circus was still being
transported from place to place by rail in 1940, but with many
improvements in the conveyances.

In Portland, Ore., I had a visit from Stanislaus Zbyszko, the
famous wrestler of preceding years. Zbyszko had worked for my
father in the Cirkus Leopold as a Greco-Roman wrestler and
strong man. He was a student at the University of Cracow then,
and I remembered him as a reader of books, as well as for his
Herculean brawn. His real name was Ziganiewicz, which is
Polish.

Our role in the Ringling Brothers and Barnum & Bailey Circus was, of course, primarily that of high-school riders, though
my own additional work as a horse trainer kept me almost continuously busy both on the road and in winter quarters. It is the
custom in the circus to turn a vicious horse or outlaw over to a
new trainer, and the great circus in Sarasota was no exception
to the rule. There was a virtual man-eater there at the time, and
I had him wished off on to me the first day. Fortunately, I expected something like that, so I took a stick of appropriate tex-
ture with me when I went into the ring. I was in the middle of
the ring when the beast was brought in and let loose. This horse
lost no time in revealing his nature, for he came at me instantly,
ears laid back, eyes ablaze with wickedness, and mouth open. I
did not retreat, but stood my ground, stick in hand. One, two,
three, the brute was upon me, and I let him have it—a rapidly

delivered and resounding crack between the ears. Down he went, to his knees, and rolled over. He had received the lesson he should have been given before. I had no further trouble with him, not the slightest, and he took his training thereafter like a good horse.

We made our high-school act in the center ring, riding the horses we had exhibited all over Europe. In Chicago I bought Charlie, a 2,000-pound Belgian, and trained him to work at liberty with Sultan, the Shetland stallion I acquired in England and brought to this country in 1940. Charlie played the part of Goliath, and Sultan the part of David. Sultan, an attractively marked piebald, was an accomplished star of the European stage and circus, and we were much attached to him. One night in Pittsburgh during the season of 1942, he came to a tragic end. While being led from the tent after the performance, something startled him and he got got away from an inattentive groom and disappeared into the darkness. An extensive search failed to reveal a trace of him. The circus left that night for Wheeling, W. Va.—without Sultan, whose body turned up the next day at Wheeling in the Ohio River, into which the pony had fallen, apparently, while on the loose the night before in Pittsburgh. Later on I had the Shetland pony Jumbo sufficiently well trained to take over the ill-fated Sultan's part in the "David and Goliath" act. Charlie and Jumbo had something in common— they both came from Chicago.

After finishing the season of 1941, we went to Cuba with Fred Bradna, who conducted a circus every winter for six weeks in the National Theatre in Havana. The Japanese attack on Pearl Harbor, which occurred while we were there, placed us in an uncomfortable position. Though we had taken the first step toward becoming citizens of the United States, we still had the status of foreigners and faced the problem, as such, of gaining re-entry at a time when the nation was at war. Bradna took our horses back to Sarasota with the circus and left us in Havana to do what we could about getting back into the United States ourselves. I was due back in Sarasota on a contract to train horses in winter quarters and was soon in default. The only consolation I had was that I couldn't do anything about it.

For four months we remained in Havana, a far from unpleasant place to be stranded in at that time, while our applications for re-entry were being processed. The procedure was complicated and involved. The applications had to go through the State Department, the War Department and the Federal Bureau of Investigation, while we went about the procurement of good behavior certificates from the police and municipal authorities of both Sarasota, Fla., and the city of Havana. Finally, on March 19, 1942, our applications were approved and visas for re-entry granted. Within three days after we got back to Sarasota, the circus train left, Manya, Dorita, and I with it, for Madison Square Garden, New York City, and the opening of the season of 1942. Alex joined the army and left for Fort Riley.

One day in 1942 a fair wind blew a prize into my path. That was the day on which I went to Ben Collins' Colonial Farm, Louisville, Ky., and bought the registered American saddle horse Colonel Washington, a bay five-year-old. There are a lot of good horses, that is true, but, as the experienced trainer and rider of high-school horses knows very well, there are not and there never were many great ones. It is one thing to be able to recognize potentiality in the raw in horses; it is another thing, and a much rarer occurrence, to discover that the horse you have under you is a great one. Not long after having acquired him, I made that discovery on the back of Colonel Washington.

The trainer and rider of high-school horses is confronted with many difficulties in this modern day, as a result of which he is frequently, if not usually, forced by circumstances, which he cannot alter, into attempting the accomplishment of too much with too many horses in too short a time. During the five years I spent in the Ringling Brothers and Barnum & Bailey Circus I trained many horses in the high-school and a lot more for liberty acts. This kept me almost constantly busy while on tour and during the winter months in Sarasota. I did not have exactly ideal conditions, therefore, under which to get along with the training of Colonel Washington. The natural aptitude of this great young horse more than made up for the disadvantages, however, and in two-and-a-half years he became as brilliant a high-school horse as I ever owned. I rode him in the center ring during my last year in the Ringling Brothers and Barnum & Bailey Circus, which was 1944, and all over the country after that at stock shows, rodeos, and special events, and in the circus.

Disaster in Hartford

Blow-downs, some of them with disastrous consequences, have been experienced by most veterans of the tenting circus, but the worst catastrophes have resulted from fires. At Schenectady, N.Y., in 1910, the Barnum & Bailey "big top" caught fire and burned. There were no casualties, but the circus sustained a heavy loss in the burning, not only of the tent, but of all its grandstand seating and equipment. We were in that one.

During our second year in the Ringling Brothers and Barnum & Bailey Circus, in 1942, a fire in the menagerie tent brought death to some 60 head of animals, among which were camels, zebras, lions, and four elephants. The horse tent was adjacent to the menagerie tent, but the horses were all evacuated in time. That was in Cleveland.

Fires like these were serious enough in terms of financial loss, but they were inconsequential as disasters when compared with the fire that destroyed the "big top" in the Ringling Brothers and Barnum & Bailey Circus at Hartford, Conn., on July 6, 1944. One hundred and sixty-nine spectators died in that fire, and hundreds more were injured, many of them severely.

As much as I would like to forget that terrible day, I know I will never be able to do so. The "big cat" act was just over, and the Wallendas were beginning to work on the high wire when it happened. Our high-school act was to come next, so we were on our horses outside the tent at the entrance, waiting. Suddenly, I saw flames at the top of the tent, on the outside of it.

After telling Manya and Dorita to take their horses away to the horse tent, and fast, I dismounted and ordered a groom to do the same with Colonel Washington. Within seconds, huge sheets of flame were everywhere within the "big top."

The audience panicked. There were screams of terror and pain as the people rushed the openings in an effort to get out, and piled up in a bone-crushing mass just short of their goal. Performers, officials, and all others of the circus personnel struggled manfully to lift the canvas at the sides, and risked their own lives dragging women and children out of the inferno. Burning canvas was falling down on the inside to add to the horror. The people on top of the piled-up humanity at the openings were dead from the searing heat and flame. Most of those under them were still alive, many of them badly injured.

As a result of this tragedy, the circus was crippled financially, and its people, from the officials and the performers on down, were all but demoralized. Conflicting testimony at the subsequent hearings on the disaster confused the issue of who was to blame. In the atmosphere that prevailed, one of shock and impatience to accuse, the disposition was to fix the responsibility almost solely on the circus officials.

The "big top" had been rainproofed with a coating of paraffin, which increased its inflammability. The canvas had not been flameproofed to begin with. But that, Robert Ringling stated, was because flameproof canvas had not been procurable because of wartime priorities. Fire-fighting apparatus in the vicinity of the circus, supposed to have been provided by the municipality, had not been so provided, it was charged. The fact that there was only one fire hydrant within a block from the circus grounds was also established. The blame was placed, however, on the circus officials, six of whom were sent to prison. The circus was fined $10,000, and, after being placed in receivership, was required to turn over the equivalent of $1,000,-000 in securities, cash, and insurance policies to the receivers in order to meet the cost of damage suits that were expected to be filed.

It was a heartsick personnel that went back to Sarasota from Hartford, and recovery was not rapid. The rest of that season's performances were made in the open air.

Farewell to My Beloved Manya

On Sept. 22, 1944, in Evanston, Ill., my good and faithful wife Manya departed this earthly life after a brief illness. I pay tribute to her as my devoted helpmate and companion without equal through the trials, tribulations, joys, and triumphs of 30 full years. I pay tribute to her also as a great horsewoman whose way with a horse was of inborn artistry, and as a daughter of the classical circus, to which she was devoted. She took up high-school riding as my pupil and became the most exceptional pupil I ever had. Only my daughter Dorita has her mother's wonderful hands. Manya's grace and style as a ballerina and bareback rider were carried over into her high-school riding. Her sense of the ballet and her instinct for the dramatic explain her conception of a high-school act, which had to be a thing of beauty. And that involved the costuming and the appointments, carried out to the nth detail. Manya was gifted in other ways: especially as a linguist. In addition to Hungarian and Russian, she spoke German, French, Italian, Spanish, Portuguese, Swedish, Danish, and English, all fluently and well. My son Alexander was overseas in Italy, in the army of Gen. Mark Clark, when his mother died. Dorita and I stayed on in the circus until the end of the 1944 season. That is the way it is and has to be in show business. And that is the way Manya would have had it.

Hurricane in Sarasota

On an otherwise uneventful day in January, 1945, in Sarasota, warnings were posted of a hurricane that was sweeping across the Gulf of Mexico toward the West Coast. Since completing the season in 1944 in the Ringling Brothers and Barnum &

Bailey Circus, I had been keeping my horses in an old riding stable not far from the winter quarters. The oncoming storm was expected to hit Sarasota during the night or in the early hours of morning, and my fears were for the safety of the horses in that old stable. There was a barn of more recent construction, and a safer one, I thought, on the other side of the city. So I hurried across town to find out if there was room for my horses there. There was not, so I had to hope for the best.

As evening came on, an ominous calm settled over the land and the sky took on a sickly glow. We had closed and secured the shutters and were as ready as we could be for the blow. Not a breath of air stirred until somewhere between 2 and 3 in the morning, when a furious wind came roaring into the void. The house quivered in the violence and, as it strained against its moorings, didn't seem to be able to make up its mind whether or not to buckle and fall apart. Torrential rains lashed at our home in such volume and with such force that at one moment I wondered if the very waters of the Gulf were not rising up from their basin to assault the land.

Not until 5 did the elements relent. As the hurricane passed on, quiet came in the path of it. After three hours of noise and pressure, the abrupt silence seemed less than soundless and made one feel light.

More than half the shingles had been torn from the roof of my house, and the upper portions of the chimneys had been blown away by the wind. The house across the street had been flattened. Fortunately, there was no one in it.

I now thought about my horses in the old riding stable and could do nothing until I knew how they were. Uprooted trees blocked the streets, so I had to go to the stable on foot. The mark of the storm was everywhere, and I feared the worst. The old riding stable, however, was unchanged from the evening before. By a seeming miracle, the winds in their full force had by-passed the place and all was well. Later in the morning I learned that the new barn, the one to which I had tried to transfer my horses, had been blown flat.

XIV

Farewell to the Wagons

Friends Have Been My Blessing

SHORTLY after the hurricane, Dorita and I went to California, having accepted a contract to ride the high-school for one year in the Russell Brothers Circus, which had been acquired by Art Concello. Opening in Los Angeles at the Pan-Pacific Coliseum, the Russell Brothers Circus became a road show, concentrating its operations on the West Coast. In the winter of 1946, we worked in Orin Davenport's Shrine Circus, and Alexander, who had returned from the war, joined us to make a threesome. That spring, Alexander and Dorita began working together, and I went to Clermont, near Indianapolis, to take up quarters and train horses.

In my voyage down through the corridor of time, 50 years of it in Europe and 20 years of it in the United States, friends have

139

been my blessing. Because of them life has been warm and gay. That is how it was during the eight months I spent in Clermont. In addition to training my own horses, I trained a few for friends, through whom I came to know many other people, not only in Clermont but in Indianapolis and other adjacent communities. Some of those whose horses I trained were members of the Indianapolis Horse Patrol, Inc., the Shrine Patrol, as it is commonly known, of the Murat Temple. An honorary life membership in that organization was presented to me by the members, and I carry it with me wherever I go. When I returned to Indianapolis a few years later, in September, 1953, to ride the high-school at the State Fair Horse Show, it was like coming home. I was appearing in an all-white spotlight act, "The White Rider," done to the strains and tempos of Franz von Suppe's "Light Cavalry Overture," and in which I rode the white Arabian Kamlah.

It seemed like home also, on succeeding occasions, when I went to Indianapolis in connection with Arthur Godfrey's exhibitions at the Horse Show on Catoctin Gold, popularly known as Goldie.

On an ill-starred night in Chicago in 1948, while in the middle of a high-school act in which Dorita and I were working together in the Polack Brothers Circus, Colonel Washington faltered and fell over dead. He was 11 years young, in full vigor and apparently in the pink. A post-mortem revealed the cause of death. He had a malformation of the heart. In losing my Colonel Washington, I lost a fortune, and knew that I might never have such a horse under me again. I wept like a child that night right there in the ring. Finishing the engagement in the Polack Brothers Circus on another horse, I rode in the circus for the last time and, in doing so, concluded a career of 60 years from the time of my birth in that world of the wagons, the tents, and bespangled wonders of the sawdust ring. With that milestone passed, I decided to settle down in Chicago. I took over the Ambassador Stable, a riding academy on the North Side, and began giving riding lessons and conducting classes.

Life has its ups and its downs, and it has been the lot of most of us, I suspect, to have had at least some acquaintance with the down-side. Perhaps it is better that way, for otherwise we might not appreciate the good fortune when it comes our way. Most of us have been not just lucky but blessed, I dare say, and I hope all of us, at some time or other. I know I have been.

I was blessed in my parents, in my brothers and sisters, on the first of October, 1914, when Manya Guttenberg became my wife. I was blessed also in my children, and not least, through all the years, in my friends. On Jan. 20, 1949, on top of so much to be grateful for, I was blessed again and blessed indeed, for on that day a lovely young lady from St. Cloud, Minn., Elizabeth Ann Murphy, and I were married.

Nan was a pupil in one of my riding classes at the Ambassador Stable. That was a dozen years ago and more, and today we live happily together with our little family of five children, Joey, aged 11; Kathy, 10; Teddy, 9; Susie, 6; and Billy, 5, in our home in Sarasota.

Bill Reichmann and Kamlah

In 1950, I moved around the block from the Ambassador to North Clark Street and that was the beginning of Arthur Konyot's Riding Academy. In the previous year, a group of Arabian horse owners of the Chicago area and other Midwestern communities put on a pageant with some 12 or more of their Arabians in connection with the International Horse Show in the International Amphitheatre at the Chicago Stock Yards. I saw it and met some of the participants, one of whom was the owner of the fine little Arabian Kamlah. Kamlah became mine, not long after that, for training, and his owner, William D. "Bill" Reichmann of Barrington, Ill., became my great friend and was later to become the narrator of these pages from my life story. This was just another chance crossing of paths, but it led to important developments.

It was not the original purpose to make a high-school horse

out of Kamlah, but that is what he became. An outwardly calm enough little horse, he had inner fires, high sensitivity, and lightning-fast reflexes. I exhibited him for the first time in June of 1950 at the first All-Arabian Horse Show of the Midwest Arabian Horse Owners, Monee, Ill., where his supreme lightness, animation, spring, and airy grace so won the hearts of the Arabian horse owners and so captured their imagination that a number of them sent me their own Arabians for training. If misconceptions and resultant misunderstandings are distressing, they are sometimes illuminating, and that was so with regard to Kamlah and the conversation he aroused as a high-schooled Arabian. Who was this European circus man who presumed to make trick horses out of Arabians, and what in the world did the owners of those Arabians think they were going to accomplish by submitting their Arabians to such training? Obviously, there was confusion.

In my riding school on North Clark Street I had a class in advanced equitation for the few who were ready for it and sufficiently interested. This was dressage and not the high-school. There were a few who wanted to go on from there and learn something about high-school riding, but that is a full bill, and not more than two or three were interested in that direction anyway. So far as the Arabians were concerned, their owners did not send them to me to be high-schooled. They sent them to me, rather, to be improved as riding horses for their own use, or to be developed for show ring competition under the rules of the American Horse Show Association for Arabians. And that is what I trained them for, with results that are of record.

The purpose of the initial training, I explained to those who sent their Arabians to me, is always the same, and that is to supple and balance the horse under the weight of the rider, which involves the coordinated functioning of the joints and muscles in the direction of lightness and elasticity of movement. This is accomplished by daily exercises until the horse is responding to the aids or controls, carrying his head well, walking on, freely, that is, and flat-footed on a light rein, trotting in balanced cadence, with increasing spring off the hocks, cantering collectedly, and changing leads smoothly and at once when prompted. When he is doing that, I explained, your horse is approaching the stage at which he may be regarded as a well-trained riding horse. You will then have the foundation—the indispensable foundation—for any further and more specialized development.

By 1951, I had from eight to a dozen Arabians in my stable. Not all of them were being trained for show, and not all of those being trained with that in mind could be winners. Enough of them did become winners, however, to etch out one fact—that they were well trained and well ridden. A difficulty was to find riders competent enough to ride a correctly trained horse in show ring competition. The best riders were my own pupils, and they were the ones who brought in the prizes. In 1952, we gave Kamlah a vacation from his high-school work, and my daughter Dorita rode him extensively in the show ring. That was quite a combination, to be sure, and proved to be practically unbeatable, especially in the major shows. The proof of the pudding, if proof there had not already been, as regards the correct training of the Arabian as a saddle horse, came in October, 1952, at the Pennsylvania National Horse Show. In that year, as before, and for several years thereafter, Arthur Godfrey sponsored the $2,000 Arabian Championship Stake and presented the trophy. Horses that had been sent to me for training were placed one, two, and three, with Dorita winning the performance championship on Kamlah. Nineteen Arabians from all over the United States competed in that class, which was judged by Ward Wells of Oswego, Ore., and it was on that night that Arthur Godfrey and I crossed paths.

Four or five months later I had a telephone call from Leesburg, Va. Who did I know in that town? Nobody. Leesburg was the place where Arthur Godfrey lived. I knew that, of course. Could it be from him? It could be, and it was. He was telephoning me, he said, to tell me he had been doing some thinking since the last Pennsylvania National and had decided to send

me some of his horses for training. A week or so later his horses
arrived at my Riding Academy in Chicago, the palomino stallion
Catoctin Gold, the Arabian stallions Sarab Al Sarah and Sunsan
and Mrs. Godfrey's Arabian mare Hunzukut. They remained
with me for a year. On the first of January, 1954, I left Chicago
with my family for Beacon Hill Farm, where I remained until
late in the spring of 1960.

The great city of Chicago will always hold a favored place in
my thoughts—first, because it was there that Elizabeth Ann
Murphy entered my life, and, second, because of the many
warm friendships formed there in that big, friendly metropolis
on the shores of Lake Michigan. It was in Chicago, moreover,
that I became identified with the training of Arabian horses.

The following letter was sent to me at the time of my departure from Chicago, and it is one that I have kept:

Dec. 7, 1953

Prof. Arthur Konyot
1508 N. Clark St.
Chicago, Illinois

Dear Pop:

In behalf of MIDWEST ARABIAN HORSE OWNERS,
I want to take this opportunity to wish you luck and God-
speed in your new venture.

We at M.A.H.O. are most grateful for the service you have
rendered in promoting interest in the ARABIAN HORSE;
and also want to thank you for the high quality of training
and horsemanship that you have conveyed to each of us.

You have set a standard for each of us to shoot at, and we
hope that each in some small measure, will exemplify your
horsemanship.

We hope that in your new location in the East, you will
think of us from time to time, and I can assure you that our
thoughts will be with you.

With kindest regards from each one of us.

Sincerely,

JACK MERVIS,
Secretary-Treasurer

XV

Oscar Konyot, Lion Trainer

The Big Cats

I LAST MENTIONED my brother Oscar in connection with his coming to North Africa in the middle 1920's to present his trick riding, roping, and bronco-busting acts in the Cirque Albert Rancy, so it is time to bring him up to date.

In 1914 Oscar was on tour in southern Italy near the Greek border in the Circo Dell'Acqua, of which he was the director. Italy went to war with Greece, and Oscar tried to persuade the Dell'Acqua brothers that they should put the circus on flat cars and head north. They wouldn't, so he parted company with them. Within a few weeks, the circus was bombed. The older of the two brothers, his wife, five children, and many of the circus personnel were killed. And that was the end of the Circo Dell'Acqua.

Signor Tongi, proprietor of the Circo Tongi, the largest circus in Italy at the present time, wanted a "big cat" act that would be outstanding. With that purpose in mind, he hired Oscar, giving him a free hand to procure the necessary animals. Meanwhile, Oscar was informed that it was Tongi's practice to put his sons in the limelight and that after having made use of a trainer he would find reason to fire him, so that the act could be turned over to one of his sons. With this information as his cue, Oscar decided to build his act around a majestic 15-year-old lion, which he bought from the zoo in Milan. Normally, this is not considered to be wise procedure, but this old lion turned out to be a veritable show in himself and the act around him became the stellar attraction of the Circo Tongi.

One fine day, Tongi came to Oscar and said:

"Lion trainer, we don't want your dog on the circus grounds." And Oscar replied: "If there is no room for my dog, Senor Tongi, there can be no room for the dog's owner."

Thereupon, he handed the keys to the cages over to Tongi and departed. This happened with a performance coming up. The son, who was taking Oscar's place, quickly donned his lion trainer's costume and got ready to show. Oscar bought a ticket to the performance and took a seat at ringside. He had a pretty good idea of what would happen, and it did happen. The majestic old lion stood against the cage door and would not let the new trainer in. There was no lion act that day. After the third day of having to take the lions out of the ring without being able to put them through their act, the owners poisoned the old lion in order to get into his cage. Tongi and his son found that they had no act, for, having been told about what they could be expected to do, Oscar had set them up for a disappointment. He had so built the act around the old lion that the rest of the lions would not show without him.

Oscar now went to Zoppe in Treviso, where he bought his own lions, some bears, and two wolves and began building an act. Before long, he received a telegram advising him of the fact that there was a special delivery letter for him at the post office, which, it transpired, was a message from the Circo Tongi asking him to return in order to train a tiger act. He replied: "I'm sorry, I still have my dog with me."

My daughter Dorita and her high-school horse Bomba, a registered American Saddle Horse.

Josephine Berosini Konyot on the high wire in the Ringling Brothers and Barnum & Bailey Circus.

My brother Oscar at Sarasota in 1952. At 62 he is still a cowboy at heart. He has favored Western regalia since the days of our American Wild West Show in Hungary.

Patricia (Mrs. Oscar) Konyot and "Konyot's Chimpanzees"—Susie, Zimba, and Sally. Oscar and Pat have traveled all over the United States, Mexico, Central and South America with this act.

Farewell to the circus world.

An extraordinary photograph of an attack by a lioness on her trainer. Oscar was passing by the cage in winter quarters at Sarasota when the animal unexpectedly reached out her left paw and grabbed his right arm, inflicting wounds that incapacitated him for several weeks.

Arthur Godfrey presents a ribbon and trophy to Dorita and William D. Reich-mann's Kamlah, winners of $2,000 Arabian Championship Stake and Farouk Challenge Trophy at Pennsylvania National at Harrisburg, Nov. 1, 1952.

My son Alexander and his high-school horse Kalarama, Jr.

Portrait by Elizabeth Bell of Dorita astride William D. Reichmann's Arabian stallion Khedive. "That horse is like silk in her hands," said a veteran horseman who saw them win the performance championship at the Third Annual All-Arabian Horse Show in Chicago in 1954.

Indianapolis is like home to me. Here I am astride Kamlah at the Indiana State Fair Horse Show in 1953.

Goldie doing a Spanish walk in good form, Arthur Godfrey in the saddle.

Doing a circus bow.

Here I am at Arthur Godfrey's Beacon Hill Farm, Leesburg, Va., teaching Catoctin Gold ("Goldie") the march step. Goldie is the horse the television star later appeared with at state fairs and horse shows all over the United States.

First lessons between the pillars. Training one of my two young Lipizzaners at Leesburg.

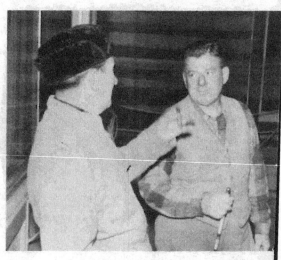

Horse talk at the Godfrey stables.

"Arthur Konyot: The White Rider," a portrait by Elizabeth Mihalyi.

Five little Konyots. My children, left to right, Billy, Susie, Teddy, Kathy, and Joey.

At Youngstown, Ohio, in 1960, where Pluto (left) and Conversano made their first public appearance.

Our family today: My wife Nan and, left to right, our children, Kathy, Susie, Billy, Teddy, and Joey.

Nobility . . . . A head study of my Lipizzaner Pluto.

The White Rider of today . . . . one of my most recent photographs.

In Zoppe, Oscar narrowly missed having his career as a lion trainer and his existence as a man cut short in the claws and fangs of an attacking lion. He had just put a new lion in the cage for a training session when the beast jumped him and wouldn't let go. He had no choice but to kill the lion or be killed himself. This was a bad beginning, and it landed him in the hospital. When he was released, he found he no longer had any animals. They had starved to death. He had paid the feed bills for them while he was in the hospital, but the animals didn't get the feed. Back at work again, he bought two more lions and a leopard and started training them, adding a lioness to the act later on. One day when he gave his cats their drinking water, only two of them, the big lion and the leopard, would drink it. Both died almost instantly. The Italian "underground," which was engaged in combative tactics against the German army, had poisoned the water. Oscar continued working with his two remaining lions and some new wolves he had acquired, but had to stop working altogether soon after that because of the almost incessant bombings as the tempo of the war accelerated. So he joined the Italian "underground."

When the war ended, he had the only remaining wild animal act in Italy, which consisted of two lions and a monkey. Every circus wanted to book him, and he made money. In 1947, after two more years on tour with this small act, the Italian government gave him the title of honorary officer of the Military Order of D'Atiochia, with the Star of Malta medal that goes with it. By 1950 he had the largest group of lions and the biggest traveling zoo in Italy. He had 24 lions and lionesses and some 80 animals of other kinds. It took two large trucks and six flat cars to transfer the animals and equipment.

On his almost yearly trips to Europe after 1946, John Ringling North sought to contract Oscar for an engagement in the United States, only to find him booked up too far in advance. For the same reason, Metro-Goldwyn-Mayer was unable to get his lions for the film *Quo Vadis* in 1950. In 1951, however, while in England for long engagements with his lion act in the London Harringay Arena and the Blackpool Tower Circus, Oscar sold his lions to North and accepted a contract.

In 1952, at Madison Square Garden in the Ringling Brothers and Barnum & Bailey Circus, Oscar worked on Good Friday to his detriment. In Europe all amusements are closed on Good Friday, excepting the moving picture theaters, which are permitted to show the Passion of Christ, and to work on this day was not in accord with Oscar's practice. On Good Friday, 1952, Menelik, one of his best performing lions and the comedian of the act, was in a mood to attack. Watching his chance, with the instinct of a wild animal in his natural domain, he waited until the final trick of the act, in which Oscar crouched behind a fence as the lionesses leaped over both the fence and himself. Menelik sat on his perch, as he was supposed to, while this went on, but the moment the last of the lionesses had hurdled the fence he sprang at Oscar, catching him under the arms with his claws and throwing him like a rag doll back and forth over the hurdle. In that performance Oscar was wearing an aluminum pith helmet, which a friend had given him only the day before. This was especially fortunate, because his head was in the lion's mouth. Despite the protection of the helmet, he would have been fatally clawed had it not been for Fanny, a pet lioness, who attacked Menelik from behind and diverted him in time, and long enough, for Oscar to escape.

After five days in the hospital, Oscar went back to the circus and his lions. The hospital refused to take the responsibility for his release, but he went anyway, patched up from head to foot. The doctor at Madison Square Garden was aghast at the sight of him, refused permission for him to go back into the arena with his lions, and placed him under his care for a week. Oscar was an exasperated and exasperating patient and spent most of the time during his confinement demanding to be released so that he could get back to the lions. Finally, the doctor relented, saying:

"All right, if you have the strength to work, you can do so. I don't think you have. Punch me in the stomach."

Oscar complied and in doing so knocked the doctor off his feet.

In 1953, in Washington, the lioness Cabieria attacked. Several times before, after leaping the hurdle and landing, she had turned with malice aforethought in attempts to attack Oscar from behind. The firing of blanks dissuaded her at first, but she lost respect for even those and changed her mind only when she got an iron stool in her face. Then came the night in Washington when Cabieria, instead of taking the hurdle, leaped with her retractile claws extended right on to Oscar's back. Though the impact of her weight bent him over and pinioned him against the hurdle, Oscar summoned enough strength to throw the beast off and to force her to her perch with his stick.

That same year in Portland, Me., during a rehearsal, the lioness Pasha lashed out in play and tore open Oscar's left arm from elbow to hand. It took 28 stitches to sew up the wide-open gash. This was the last of a total of 54 such injuries. Oscar finished the season of 1954 with Ringling and, thereafter, bought the first of his chimpanzees. A telegram from Clyde Beatty resulted in an 18-week engagement presenting the Beatty lions, at the conclusion of which Oscar gave up the big cats for good and returned to Sarasota and the training of his chimpanzees in earnest.

The Konyot Chimpanzees

Oscar opened with his chimps in Havana on Dec. 3, 1954, and, accompanied by his young wife Pat, a dancer, toured the interior of Cuba, showing at sugar centrals. The tent was pitched at sugar cane weighing-in stations, lonely places during the day, with no one there and nothing happening. At night, however, whole families of sugar cane workers, led by a man carrying a machete, would converge on the station from the plantations and fill the tent to overflowing. After about three and one half months of this in Cuba, Oscar, Pat, and the chimps went to Nicaragua, where they put up with a complex of hardships, such as heat, dirt, poor food, and bad sanitation, that tested the soul.

They had to bathe from a bucket, using a coconut shell as a
dipper. With relief, they went from Nicaragua to San Jose, the
capital of Costa Rica and a fine city, and from there took a rice
boat to South America. The port of destination was Buena Ventura, Colombia, and the voyage was supposed to take about two
days. Instead, it took 18 days. The captain of the ship, it seemed,
had lost his direction. There was no cook on board, and no food,
so Oscar decided to do some fishing. He used an old shirt as bait
and caught three tuna among other fishes, which the crew ate
raw. One of the tuna pulled away with such force on the line
that Oscar suffered a badly burned and wrenched hand.

This was voyaging of a very unhappy kind. Pat and Oscar
shared the only cabin on the boat with an elephant man and his
wife. The sea was running high and the old rice boat tossed
around like a cork and shipped a lot of water, which sloshed
back and forth on the deck and on the floor of the cabin. The floor
of the cabin had been freshly painted with a red water paint,
which dissolved in the sea water. Everything became red, including the elephant man's dog. The poor dog was terrified by the
pitching of the ship, so he jumped on to the two bunks alternately,
joining his master and mistress in their bunk and Oscar and Pat
in theirs. The bedding became red, along with everything else.

From Buena Ventura, Oscar and Pat took a trip across the
mountains on a daylong journey to Cali. The road was a mere
trail, and a very winding one, cut into the mountain walls. Crosses
studded the edge of the mountain-spiraling road at disturbingly
numerous points, grimly calling one's attention to fatal occur-
rences. Whenever the bus came to a stop the passengers got out
and lit candles to petition for a safe journey.

Oscar made his chimp act for a period of four weeks in Cali,
where he and Pat luxuriated in warm running water, soap, and
the other comforts of a good hotel. A similarly comfortable stay
in Bogota, for eight weeks, came next, and the Oscar Konyots
actually had pasteurized milk in that city. Sally, a rollicking one-
year-old chimp which they had bought somewhere else for later
delivery, came to them in Bogota in a Pan American plane. That,

of course, was a happy event, but the pleasure it occasioned was more than dampened a week later by the onslaught of a great sadness. Tommy died.

Tommy was more than just a big, winsome, and typically clever performing chimp. The extent to which he put himself into his work was exceptional and made him rare. He never flagged, not even when he was a really sick chimp. Oscar had been treating him toward the last, just as he would have treated an unwell child. He took him to a pediatrician and, when his breathing became labored, to a lung specialist. Tommy had become so accustomed to undergoing blood tests that he didn't flinch when the needle was inserted. He was so understanding that, without prompting, he held the cotton in place himself when the needle was withdrawn. But now it was all over. Poor Tommy was dead. Oscar bought a coffin for him that had been designed for a 15-year-old child and, accompanied by Pat and a doctor friend, took it in a taxicab into the mountains for burial. This was not the last that would be heard of the small coffin and what it contained, however.

The native Colombian who drove Oscar, Pat, and the entourage into the mountains with the coffin had the makings of a detective—or imagined he had. A chimpanzee in that coffin? How did he know there was? Maybe the Americanos had murdered somebody and were taking the body of the murdered person into the lonely mountains in that coffin? The man gave no indication of his suspicion to Oscar and Pat. But he did communicate the dark thought to the newspapers back in Bogota, with the result that the awful possibility was spelled out in headlines the next day. It was a rash surmise, of course, if not an absurdity, and it fell flat in a hurry. Nevertheless, the excitement those headlines aroused was extensive, and no doubt a great many people were secretly disappointed when their anticipation of some macabre revelations was not sustained.

Upon the death of Tommy, Susie snapped out of her spoiled child ways and gave up the antics she had been prone to in the midst of a performance. Within a week she had learned a sufficient number of new stunts and tricks to take Tommy's place in the act and from then on became a star. Back in Sarasota, Fla., again, after the termination of the South American tour with a few engagements in Venezuela, the three-year-old Zimba joined the act.

In training Pat to present his performing chimps, Oscar has had an apt pupil. From a background of experience as a dancer and show girl in her native England, and in France in the Folies Bergere, Patricia came to the United States in 1953, and shortly thereafter became a dancer and show girl in the Ringling Brothers and Barnum & Bailey Circus. Trained by Oscar and presented by the talented, ever graceful, and beautifully costumed Pat, the Konyot chimpanzees have a repertoire of acrobatics and drolleries that make the act one of the best by performing Simians in this or any other country.

XVI

Trainer for Arthur Godfrey

IN THE FIRST conversation I ever had with him, which was over the long distance telephone in February, 1953, Arthur Godfrey told me of his interest in dressage and of his wanting to learn how to ride a dressaged or high-schooled horse. Before the year was up, with that objective in view, he hired my services as a horse trainer and instructor of equitation.

I took up residence on Beacon Hill Farm at Leesburg, Va., in the first month of 1954, but my famous pupil-to-be did not begin to take lessons until the following summer. This was because of the delicate hip operation he had undergone during the summer of the preceding year and his doctor's orders to refrain from riding for a prescribed period of time.

Here was a man who really loved to ride. Ever since his automobile accident of a few years before he had suffered severe pain after a short time in the saddle. Yet he kept on riding. His

153

condition had improved somewhat, but he still had to use a cane and had to be assisted into the saddle. Few men in his condition would have aspired as he did, and it would have been understandable if he had decided to give up riding altogether. Not only did he persevere, however, but, adhering to his purpose, he accomplished his riding in the face of a physical handicap and did so in a remarkably short time. In view of the fact that the full schedule and many activities and interests of the famous radio and television personality left him only the weekends for riding lessons and practice, he would have done well if he had learned how to put Goldie through his routine as proficiently as he did in twice the time.

The Godfrey version of a high-school act was his own and involved the use of a microphone worn under the vest and the services of the skilled sound engineer, Richard Whitman. Those who saw the act, and innumerable thousands in the United States and Canada did, will remember the rider as he came smilingly into the ring in this talking high-school act on his white-bridled, fluidly moving horse, a dark palomino with flaxen mane, forelock and tail. Previously more at home in a high-backed Western saddle, he was now relaxed and correctly positioned in the flat saddle of international usage.

"Ladies and gentlemen," he would say. "I want to introduce you tonight to my horse Goldie. Goldie is a palomino stallion, etc."

The voice, which was amplified, was conversational and the effect was to create an informal atmosphere, in which a state of rapport between the man on the horse and the onlookers was quickly achieved. It is doubtful if anyone ever attempted this sort of thing before, and it took the personality of Arthur Godfrey to put it over. There is little familiarity with high-school riding in this country and the informal manner in which Godfrey explained what he was doing proved effective. Cueing the horse into the various movements of the high-school routine or into the performance of such accomplishments as mounting the pedestal, bowing down, nodding his head for yes and shaking it for no, etc., he commended him when he did well and took the blame himself when he didn't. It was a new kind of showmanship and with Arthur Godfrey in the saddle it proved popular.

The act was introduced at the Loudoun County Horse Show in Leesburg in the summer of 1955 and came into its own in the fall of that year with exhibitions at the Pennsylvania National in Harrisburg and the International in Madison Square Garden, New York. In 1956 there were horse show dates in Leesburg, Upperville, and Warrenton, Va., return dates at the Pennsylvania National and the International at New York, and new dates at the Indiana State Fair Horse Show in Indianapolis and the Toronto Royal Winter Fair in Canada. The 1957 itinerary was even more extensive, taking the act to Omaha's Ak-Sar-Ben, by air to San Diego from Baltimore and back, to the Cow Palace in San Francisco, to Madison Square Garden, New York, and to the International Live Stock Exposition and Horse Show in Chicago.

As the trainer of the horse for this role and as the man who was teaching the rider how to put the horse through his routine, it was necessary that I be present at all these shows. And I journeyed to a number of places on the itinerary in advance of the engagements to make sure that accommodations were being provided for and arrangements were being carried out as promised. The organization and management of a great horse show adds up to a complicated business and requires a whole corps of experienced hands to be accomplished smoothly. Horse show managements have the best of intentions, of course, but sometimes have to be prodded into acting upon them. We succeeded, on the whole, in getting the accommodations we needed and were invariably treated with the utmost kindness and consideration. An exacting matter was the protection of the radio and television celebrity against over-eager fans and admirers. This required extra police details and the cooperation of the state police at the state fairs. Autograph seekers and others tried to gain admission to our quarters and had to be dissuaded adroitly.

The much publicized Goldie had to be removed from view. Had he not been the crowds would have blocked off all access to his stall by the groom and caretaker.

Still enthusiastic over his exhibitions on Goldie, which had proved well worth the while financially in 1957, Arthur Godfrey embarked on and carried out an equally extensive itinerary in 1958. In that year, in addition to repeat engagements in Indianapolis, Toronto, and Chicago, we exhibited at the Eastern States Exposition in Springfield, Mass., the Kentucky State Fair Horse Show in Louisville, and the New Mexico State Fair in Albuquerque, going to New Mexico by air as far as Denver, the rest of the way by truck.

That summer we came back to Chicago, this time to the Shrine Convention, at which Arthur Godfrey presented Goldie in the ballroom of the Hotel Sherman and rode him in the great Shrine parade in Soldier Field, where he was awarded the "Horseman of the Year" trophy, a 50-pound silver cup. The trophy was presented by the governor of Illinois, William G. Stratton.

When I went to Beacon Hill Farm in January, 1954, the Godfreys were Arabian horse enthusiasts. Mrs. Godfrey had been riding Hunzukut alongside big horses of Thoroughbred hunter type in the hunts but had become more interested in competing with her in the show ring in the Arabian performance classes. This she did successfully for several years, after which she retired the little mare to the quieter life of a broodmare. Thereafter, a beautiful gray stallion of classic mold, Alyfar, was acquired from the Kellogg Unit of the California State Polytechnic College, Pomona, to be trained for show ring performance and to be used in the stud. Alyfar is an Arabian of outsanding excellence and, though her interest in show riding and in Arabian horses had waned considerably, Mrs. Godfrey did well enough with him in performance to win several performance grand championships, one of which was at the International Horse Show in Madison Square Garden, New York, in 1956. The Godfreys lost interest in their Arabian horses together several years ago. Sarab Al Sarah, with which we won another grand championship in Madison Square Garden, was disposed of first, then Sunsan, Godfrey's first Arabian, and, finally, just prior to my departure in June, 1960, Alyfar. The interest had become focused on the racing string. The hunters remained. At length the race horses were dispersed, and Beacon Hill went Western.

Not all of my work on Beacon Hill Farm was with horses. A Sicilian donkey, Pete the monkey, the miniature French poodle Chippy, and even an elephant became my charges, to be trained for television appearances. Aside from these, the horses, and Hereford cattle in sizeable numbers, there were other animals at Beacon Hill. But they did not come within my province. The deer and elk and a few buffalo were confined to the parks. Beautiful peafowl graced the lawns and a pair of Mexican donkeys made themselves heard when they could not be seen. In 1957, not long after our engagement in San Diego with Goldie, a very stately white llama arrived as a gift from San Diego's Balboa Park Zoo, to be joined later on by a mate, the gift of friends. The two were quartered in a box stall in the stable with the hunters, where they became a center of attraction. The llamas were potential trainees, but the accent was now on things Western.

Helali, the elephant, was from Pakistan, and had been sent to Godfrey as a gift. When she arrived in New York I was on hand to meet her and to take her by truck to Leesburg. She had been described as a baby, but when I saw her I knew she was a six- or seven-year-old. In short, she was a whale of a baby, far more massive and heavier than the biggest of draft horses. School days soon began for her, with a session almost every day. She liked attention almost as much as she liked apples, but her first lessons not so well. Elephants are sociable animals and they are inclined to grieve when separated from their own. So Helali's was probably a case of a very big little girl wishing she was back with her kind in the sand lot in Pakistan. Her caretakers, and my assistants during the training sessions, were the colored grooms and stable boys, to whom an elephant was a whole lot of unknown quantity and a creature to be approached warily or not to be approached at all. Several times Helali got away from them and, dashing into the woods, disappeared in the underbrush. She was not easy to retrieve. As the spring of 1960 rolled around she was learning her lessons well and gave promise of becoming a real performer. But by that time Beacon Hill Farm had taken on the aspect of a Western stock ranch and my work was finished. Helali will probably be going to a circus, if not to a zoo, in which event she will have the company of other elephants, and that should make her happy.

XVII

Horses in the Circus

The Horse of the Bareback Riders

SINCE THE bareback act of modern times usually involves a group of from four to ten riders, with the horse having to carry all of them at once at some point during the act, the horse has to be a big, sturdy animal. His function is that of a moving platform and springboard for the vaulting, somersaulting riders, so he must have a broad back and comparatively long, wide, and level quarters. Typically, therefore, he is of draft type, weighing from 1,400 to 1,550 pounds. The acrobatics of the bareback rider are a matter of split-second timing to the movement of the horse, so the horse must be trained to canter and gallop around the ring with the utmost steadiness at an unvarying pace. His movement must be straight-going and smooth, with just the right amount of spring, and he must have a good natured, even-tempered disposition. It takes a full year to train a horse for this work and only a small percentage of the horses taken up and put to train-

159

ing develop into reliable mounts. Too many are prone to shying or kicking or prove ticklish over the loins. Some are not smooth enough in their way of going. It is customary to apply powdered resin to their backs and quarters, so that the riders will have a firmer footing, which explains why the bareback horses are sometimes referred to as resinbacks. The resin is applied just before the act and brushed out after it. We used to put moistened sawdust on the backs and quarters under a sheet or cover and we left it there overnight to absorb the resin that had eluded the brush.

There were some great names in the ranks of the bareback riders in my day. Marasso, Orin Davenport, Fred Derrick, Enrico Caroli, Ernest Clarke, Hubert Cooke, James and Claude Powell, Hipoli Houcke, a Hungarian by the name of Parker, Mable O'Brien, Lucy Belli, Sefta Loyal, Hulda Carre, and Ella Bradna come quickly to mind. May Worth, the Australian, has never had an equal as a somersaulter among the women and few among the men. Charlie Siegrist, probably the greatest all-around acrobatic performer of record, was one of the best, and I must not forget the Negro, Arthur Wacker, long famous in Europe as a *voltigeur*. There were some notable bareback riding families, the Lucuson, Casi, and Reinsch families, and, more recently the Hanaford, Loyal Repinski, and Cristiani families.

The Training of the Liberty Horses

The education or training of the horse at liberty is older than the modern circus, and it is recorded that up until about 200 years ago horse trainers with the ability to induce this kind of obedience were believed to have the powers of the sorcerer or magician, and some of them were burned alive for being so possessed. The Neapolitan Pietro, for example, was consigned to the flames, together with his little horse Mauraco, in the public market place. Fortunately for the succeeding generations, the trainer of the horse at liberty was long ago emancipated from the charge of witchcraft, and the liberty act, when performed to perfection by a group of harmoniously fine horses under the presentation of a skilled trainer, came into its own as an attraction, that never fails to cast a magic spell.

The horses in a liberty act can be of any breed or of mixed breeding and are usually of a refined type, weighing around 1,000 to 1,100 pounds. There are exceptions to this rule, of course, and I myself have trained draft horses for this kind of work. Since the horses in a liberty act are exhibited in groups of six, eight, 12, and sometimes 16 or 18 and even 24, they should be uniform in size and type and attractive in appearance. As to whether it is more effective for an act to be made up of horses of the same color, that depends on what kind of an act the trainer wants to make with them. Dissimilarities in color should be balanced, however.

The common notion that the cracking of the *chambriere*, or whip, guides and governs the horses in their movement is incorrect. Certain motions by the trainer and movements he makes with his *chambriere* are what a group of liberty horses respond to in the course of their routine, and the only effect the cracking of the *chambriere* has on them is to induce them to go forward.

A group of liberty horses can be presented after six months of training, but the horses are not dependable until they have been in training for a year. A good liberty horse trainer must be a man of ideas; he must have imagination and ingenuity. Otherwise, the act is likely to be mechanical and dull, which it never is when it is the product of a master—of such masters of the art, to cite some of the greatest I have known, as the Renz family, the Schumanns, Petoletti, Sr., Henrico and Lulu Gautier, Albert Carre, Edward Wolf, Sr., and Czeslaw Mraczkowsky. Perhaps I should not fail to mention William Truzzi of the Russian circus, who made an outstanding liberty act in conjunction with his "Thousand and One Nights," an equestrian fantasy which involved 50 horses.

The Art of the High-School Horse

The aristocrat of circus horses is the high-school horse, indeed, as the art of *haute école* training and riding stems directly from the Riding School, which was the exclusive patronage of the Royal and Imperial Courts. With the advent of the modern era, the masters of the art had no choice but to go out before the public with their wonderfully trained horses and their own ability as exhibitionists to earn a living. When superbly executed, as in the finest classical tradition, a coordinated routine in the "airs" of the *haute école* or high-school is the full flowering of an art deriving from the days of chivalry, perfected in the Court Riding Schools, and preserved since then, usually under the very opposite of ideal circumstances, by the few who have devoted their lives to it.

A horse does not become a high-school horse simply because he has been trained to bow or lie down, to sit on his haunches, or to mount a pedestal. These are nice little accomplishments that entertain a great many people, but they belong to the school of tricks and have nothing to do with that higher reach in equestrian performance which is the high school. Most high-school riders, myself among them, frequently do some of these things in the course of an exhibition, and they do so for the compelling reason that it is the public they have to please, and the public likes them.

An adept and fully trained high-school horse will do the collected and extended trot, the collected canter, the change of leads at every fourth and third step, at every other step, and at every step, which is called the flying change. He will trot on the oblique, two-track, do the shoulder-in and shoulder-out, the serpentine and *traversade, pirouette, piaffe,* and *passage.* The fully developed high-school horse will also do such things as the one-step, three-step and march, the canter in place, the canter on three legs, the backward canter and trot and the *balancier.* Contemporary writers on the subject of dressage, who may or may not be accomplished in the advanced phases of equitation they write about, have inveighed against certain of these above-mentioned "airs" on the ground that they are unnatural and serve no useful purpose in the development of the horse as the ultimate in a responsive, controllable, and versatile mount. The experienced high-school trainer and exhibitionist would be the first to concede that not all the "airs" of the high school are useful in the training and development of the horse for any other purpose, though many, if not most of them, are, and beyond dispute. It is a labored point, however, for the reason that the high school, in contradistinction to dressage, as such, is an end in itself and must be judged accordingly. There is good high school and bad, and between the good and the bad there is a wide gulf. Good high school, by which I mean the best, can be likened to the ballet, which in its ultimate form is an end in itself and its own justification accordingly. The high school is exhibition.

It takes many years of a man's life to become skilled in the training and exhibition of high-school horses, and the high-school rider, like anyone else, has to earn his bread and butter. He is not eligible, because he is a professional, to compete in the dressage events of the Olympic Games, but that cannot concern him greatly, because he knows that if he were to exhibit horses within the restricted requirements of Olympic dressage, he would starve to death.

There is no mistaking a finely trained, expertly ridden high-school horse. The grace, elasticity and lightness of step which he describes throughout will delight the eye. Self-impelled seemingly, in opposition to his rider never, he is the picture of vigor and animation. An evenly maintained cadence and fluidity of movement will be the mark of him in every "air" and in the transitions from one "air" to another. His impulsion from the quarters and off the hocks will be pronounced, his action at the trot forward-springing, and at full extension he will give the impression of being on air. On the bit always, neither ahead of it nor behind it, he will be as flexible as satin under his rider, coming readily to hand from extension to collection, shortening his paces without change of cadence and becoming elevated as he does so. At highest collection, with his resources fully assembled, he will do the *piaffe*, which is the trot in place, and from the *piaffe* he will move forward, going straight, with no perceptible swinging of the hips, into a soaring, rhythmic, and beautifully accented *passage*.

This, in brief, is the high-school horse, an impression, that is, though only a slight one, of a real high-school horse under a necessarily skilled rider. In a book on the training of animals in general, with special emphasis on the training of horses, which is now only in the planning stage, it will be my purpose to treat with the subject of dressage and the high-school in a clarifying and illuminating manner.

The Circus in the United States Today

It would be an understatement to say that all is not well with circus folk in the United States today. For the plain fact is that a feeling of discouragement so afflicts the circus families in this country that a growing number of circus parents are losing the desire to have their children follow in their footsteps.

There are a number of reasons for this situation and a basic one is the matter of pay. Circus *astistes* in most of the larger circuses in the United States are being paid about what their forebears received 50 years ago, but in depreciated dollars. In terms of what the dollar will buy, therefore, they are getting less today, and much less. To make matters worse, they are presently being paid pro rata, only for the days on which there is a performance, that is, with no pay for the time consumed en route, whereas they used to be paid by the week.

As a result of disturbed conditions following the war it was easier than it was in former years to attract the talent of European and other countries, in consequence of which the market became overcrowded with *artistes* from abroad. This was so for a long time. Nevertheless, the agencies brought in more talent every year, even though, as they know, few new outlets were opening up for the increasing numbers. Fifty years ago there were many more circuses in the United States than there are today, many of them of large size, and the *artistes* could find lucrative employment as well in the vaudeville theatres, of which there were a great many. All that is now gone. The agencies have been in a position to take advantage of the situation and they have been doing so. What it all adds up to is that circus *artistes* in the United States have not been making much more than a bare living. That being so, they have not been able to help each other as they used to. The preservation of all the exacting skills of circus performance, which depends on continuity from generation to generation within the circus families, is being encouraged by a far better condition in the European circus, but in this country it is in jeopardy.

Epilogue

Looking Backward and Looking Forward

This brings my story up to the present. In a career that has had wide dimensions in time and in place, I have traversed the distances, many thousands of miles, in the wagons, by rail, by ship, by automobile and plane. Show business has taken me to three continents and 19 countries, to the Azores in the middle of the Atlantic and the island of Madeira. My 60 years in the circus were lived through critical times, in sunlight and shadow, through wars and revolutions, in storm and stress. There was some heavy going along the way. The skies clouded over and lightning flashed. But the storms passed, and in the wake of them there was always a rainbow. The wars came. They took their toll and left their blight. But life went on.

The circus has nothing to do with war and politics. It has endured them and suffered ruin, but it usually survived. By what demons are the people of the circus possessed, I have heard it asked, that they should be so indestructible? That is something I never thought about. I can only speak for myself. I just met things as they came. A man does best what he knows how to do, and his best is never too good. So far as the circus is concerned, it is the public that decides, in the last analysis, and it is the response of the public that has kept the circus going. The circus sings the song of life. Delighting the young and refreshing the old, it appeals to those components of human nature that are not measured by the demarcations of time or the distances that separate, which makes it perennial. As entertainment, the circus is a universal medium. That is why it has survived so much for so long and why it will survive all. Farewell.

167

Glossary

Aerialist—An acrobat who works in the air on rigging suspended from the upper part of the tent or circus structure.

Ballerina On Horseback—An *equestrienne*, traditionally in tights and tarlatans, who performs acrobatics and assumes graceful postures on the back of a cantering horse.

Catcher—The "catcher" is the partner of the "flyer" in the technique of the aerialist. On releasing himself from the swinging trapeze, the flyer stretches out his arms and flies into the arms of his catcher, after having performed one of the somersaults while in mid-air. The two grasp each other at the elbows.

Collected Trot—At the collected trot the strides are shorter than at the ordinary trot, the forehand is elevated, the neck is more arched and carried more upright. Perfection at the collected trot is a mark of the well dressaged horse, and especially of the finished high-school horse. The hocks are lifted airily and engaged well under the mass. The horse moves with lightness of step, with elasticity and verve.

Dressage—A word of French origin, which means the training of domesticated animals. In application to horses, *dressage* is a universally subscribed to, time-tested system and method of training and riding the saddle horse with the objective of developing him into a highly obedient, flexible and efficient mount.

Ecuyere—The French term for a female equestrian performer.

Entree Clown—One of the clowns that make their appearance at the opening of the show.

169

El Grande Circo Ecuestre—Spanish for Great Equestrian Circus.

Flyer—An aerialist who performs on the flying trapeze.

Flying Trapeze—One of the swinging trapezes of the aerialist, which hang from above at a sufficient distance apart to enable the flyer to propel himself through the air from one trapeze to the other. In addition to the trapezes, the aparatus of the "flying" aerialists consists of a small platform, which hangs below the trapeze, plus rings or holds.

Haute Ecole—The French term, of international usage, for the highest and ultimate training of the dressaged horse. The movements or exercises of the *haute ecole* are called "airs." Many of these "airs" are considered to be natural to the horse. Others are not. Certain of the "airs" that are commonly performed by professional exhibition riders come within the latter category.

In the heyday of equestrianism the schooled horses were trained to settle back on their haunches from a rear, in an almost sitting posture, as a prelude to the performance of one of a series of leaps forward into the air. These are known as "figures off the ground," whereas the other "airs" of the *haute ecole* are classified as "figures on the ground." The "figures off the ground" are performed to a methodical perfection at the *Spanische Hofreitschule* in Vienna, Austria. The initial position is the *levade*. In the *mezair,* the horse advances from the *levade* position in successive hops or jumps. The leaps into the air are the *courbette, croupade, ballotade* and *capriole.*

High School—Same as *haute ecole.*

Jockey Act—A bareback act in which the emphasis is on a display of vaulting, from the ground to the moving horse and back again, and from horse to horse, by riders in jockey uniforms.

Liberty Act—An act in which horses without riders—literally, at liberty—perform in groups of 6, 8, 12, 16 and sometimes as many as 24. The act is presented by the trainer, traditionally in formal attire, who carries a long whip, as he directs the group in a routine of rhythmically executed figures at the trot and canter, with variations and innovations, according to his skill and ingenuity.

Lipizzaner— The commonly used name for the Lipizzan, the famous Austrian breed of horses, most of them grays, turning white early, which is known to the world in connection with the *Spanische Hofreitschule* in Vienna, where they are trained to a classical perfection in the *haute ecole*.

Manoeuvre and Quadrille—The simulation of human dancing formations by one or more groups of from 5 to 20 mounted horsemen and horsewomen, a favorite and featured exercise of the European riding halls.

March—A showy march or parade step, also known as the Spanish walk, in which the horse raises and puts his forelegs down in a slashing manner in 4, 3, and 2 beat time to music. The march steps are pure exhibition and as such are regularly included in the routine of most high-school riders.

Parforce **Rider**—A traditional European term for an equestrian acrobat who performs feats of trick riding on a fast-galloping horse in the circus. Many of the best *parforce* riders have been of Russian origin.

Passage—A slow, stately, distinctly cadenced and very elastic trot, in which the horse lifts his diagonal legs and feet with an accentuated flexion of hock and knee and with a pronounced lithesomeness of step moves forward over the ground as though on springs. The passage is accented at the apex of each soaring stride with a brief but visible suspension or delay in the action, at which point, as if freed of his earthly weight, the horse seems about to take wing.

Pedestal—A small barrel or tub, which the circus-trained horse is taught to mount with one foreleg and in that position to pivot. The top of the barrel, on which the horse balances with one foreleg, turns.

Perch Pole—A pole used by acrobats in the circus for climbing and balancing acts.

Piaffe—The trot in place, in which the horse is marking time and not moving forward. He is at highest collection. The *piaffe* is an "air" of the high-school.

Pirouette—The pivot on the hocks of the high-school.

Pyramid—A pair of bareback horses are cantering around the ring abreast, carrying 4 riders. Each horse has a rider on his back, the riders standing. A third rider is positioned between numbers 1 and 2, straddling the pair of horses. The fourth balances on the shoulders of 1 and 2, centering the formation. This is a pyramid. Pyramids involving 4 and 5 horses and 8 riders are not uncommon.

Voltigeur—A bareback rider whose special skill is that of a vaulter.

OF THIS FIRST EDITION 1,500 COPIES WERE PRINTED AND BOUND AT THE PLIMPTON PRESS, LA PORTE, INDIANA. THE TEXT IS SET IN CALE-DONIA LINOTYPE WITH MONOTYPE CASLON HEAD-INGS. TYPOGRAPHY AND BINDING DESIGN BY VAN ALLEN BRADLEY.

CPSIA information can be obtained
at www.ICGtesting.com
Printed in the USA
BVHW010920280521
608372BV00012B/107